CW00956896

100 Ideas for
Early Years Practitioners

School Readiness

Clare Ford

BLOOMSBURY

Published 2014 by Bloomsbury Education

Bloomsbury Publishing plc

50 Bedford Square, London, WC1B 3DP

www.bloomsbury.com

978-1-4729-0384-6

A CIP record for this publication is available from the British Library.

1 3 5 7 9 10 8 6 4 2

Typeset by Fakenham Prepress Solutions, Fakenham, Norfolk, NR21 8NN

Printed by CPI Group (UK) Ltd, Croydon, CR0 4YY

This book is produced using paper that is made from wood grown in managed, sustainable forests. It is natural, renewable and recyclable. The logging and manufacturing processes conform to the environmental regulations of the country of origin.

To see our full range of titles visit www.bloomsbury.com

Contents

Acknowledgements

With huge thanks to Hannah and all the other wonderful and inspirational people I have worked with in schools over the past 20 years; to my brother, Paul, who gave me the push to begin writing and encouraged me to persevere; to Holly, Jen and the team at Bloomsbury for their help and support; to my mum and dad, Jan and Mike, who listened so well; and, of course, to my patient and tolerant family, Jeremy, Harry and Maisie.

Introduction

Early Years settings are busy, exciting (and sometimes tiring!) places to work. As young minds and bodies leap from one activity to the next, there is a constant need for new and creative ideas that will engage and stimulate the young learner.

Early Years practitioners are increasingly asked to justify their work; the play provision, the adult role and the physical environment all contribute to the development of each individual child. This is not easy when faced with an army of small children, at different stages of development emotionally, physically and academically.

By the end of their time in Early Years, all children need to be ready for school, regardless of their different starting points. They will need to develop many fundamental and foundational skills while in your care. We all know that observation is the key to spotting how we can help children to develop, and this book can help you to find novel and stimulating ways to identify and nurture your children's emerging abilities.

This book is intended to be used by teachers, TAs and play workers in Early Years environments. It may be used as part of the long or medium term planning process, giving ideas for the development of an area of learning. Equally, it may be used to address short-term issues. It is not intended to be read cover-to-cover, but as a handy resource to be dipped into.

The book explores ideas relating to all key learning areas, for example:

- Self-help skills, routines and behaviour.
- Sensory and physical development.
- Fine motor skills.
- Literacy.
- Mathematical understanding.
- Communication.
- Creativity.

All the ideas are intended to be fun and motivating and the majority need minimal preparation. Most will only require the use of basic resources that are commonly found in Early Years settings and aim to reduce rather than increase your workload.

I hope you enjoy using the book in your setting as much as I have enjoyed compiling the ideas. Remember that our role is to teach, not to test, and by providing inspiring and interesting activities the act of learning is made as fun as possible.

How to use this book

This book includes quick, easy, practical ideas for you to dip in and out of, in order to prepare the children in your setting for school and their next stage of life.

Each idea includes:

- A catchy title, easy to refer to and share with your colleagues.
- A quote from a practitioner or child describing their experiences of the idea.
- A summary of the idea in bold, making it easy to flick through the book and identify an idea you want to use at a glance.
- A step-by-step guide to implementing the idea.

Each idea also includes one or more of the following:

Teaching tip

Practical tips and advice for how and how not to run the activity or put the idea into practice.

Taking it further

Ideas and advice for how to extend the idea or develop it further.

Bonus idea

There are 28 bonus ideas in this book that are extra exciting, extra original and extra interesting.

Involving parents

Tips for how to get parents involved in their child's learning, either in the Early Years setting or at home.

Settling in

Part 1

One of a kind

"The children are all so different. That's what makes it fun!"

Every child's experiences at home, the influence and expectations of their family and friends and their culture and perhaps religion, will have an impact on them as an individual.

An Early Years environment needs to reflect and promote the diversity of the community. Each child will think and respond to experiences in a different way. Children need to learn to recognise and accept the similarities and differences between themselves and others.

- Allow choices to be made during activities. Some children will need to be encouraged to make decisions but there is no reason that every child should produce an identical model or follow the same route around an adventure play area.
- Take note of any interests a child may have and build on these. For example, if a child brings in a book about frogs then you could create a pond in the water tray, an outdoor jumping trail, or sing 'Five Speckled Frogs'.
- Celebrate the differences between families. Include examples from your own home life when making comparisons.
- Draw attention to the different choices that children make. 'Harry chose to paint his boat red and Maisie chose blue. They both look lovely.'
- Use conversations about differences to include children with SEN. A learning or language difficulty should be accepted in a similar way to a different religion.
- Ensure that the resources reflect the diversity of your cohort and local community. Provide cooking utensils and play food that will be familiar, diverse dressing-up clothes for boys and girls and a variety of books with illustrations that promote inclusion.

Involving parents

Parents may be willing to come to your setting to show things that demonstrate their individuality. They may show an unusual pet, hold a conversation in a language other than English with their child, talk about a festival or celebration, share special foods or play an unusual instrument. The interest that you show will model the inclusive attitude that we hope to instil in children.

Help me!

"Sometimes he just cries. I always check he's not hurt and then try to give him a drink or fruit. It's a guessing game!"

The adult to child ratio in an Early Years setting usually makes it possible to anticipate and attend to the needs of young children. In a mainstream school classroom there will be a greatly reduced ratio. Children will need to be able to ask for help, wash and dry their hands, attend to their own toileting needs etc.

In order to develop self-help skills, children must first recognise a need, then identify the action that is necessary to meet that need and evaluate whether this is something that can be managed independently or requires assistance. They then need to take that action or communicate their need to an appropriate person. With so many steps, it's not as straightforward as it initially seems!

- If it becomes clear that a child is not able to meet their own needs or ask for support, try to establish the stage at which the child is having difficulties. Discuss your thoughts with your SENCO. For example, the child may be unaware that they are too hot and therefore not aware that removing a jumper will solve this. They may also be unable to physically remove their own jumper or unable to form the words or signs to ask an adult for help.
- Support individuals at the necessary stage by modelling, describing and using hand over hand support if necessary. Then reduce support and praise success, however small.
- Many Early Years settings have areas where children pour themselves a drink when thirsty. These are fantastic for promoting independence in most children, but need to be monitored, as there may be some children who never take a drink.

- Discuss individual children's self-help abilities regularly and establish a consistent approach from all adults. It won't take a child who is reluctant to attempt a task independently long to find the one soft hearted Early Years worker who can't say no!
- If children are finding it difficult to communicate their needs, have symbol cards available to them. A picture of a cup or toilet can give the child the voice they need to ask for assistance.
- When reading stories or playing alongside children in role-play areas, draw attention to a character's needs and encourage a child to find the solution.
- Highlight your own needs and encourage children to find the solution. For example, 'I'm really thirsty' may be met with a pretend cup of tea or could develop into a discussion about favourite drinks. Either way, it draws attention to a need and solution.
- When difficulties are identified, discuss these with the child's parents. Is the situation the same at home? Is the child encouraged to attempt tasks independently? Is the child finding it difficult to communicate with less familiar adults?

Taking it further

Talk to schools that regularly receive children from your setting. Ask which skills they find to be lacking or most useful. Target these for focussed work.

Bonus idea ★

Use decorated stickers that say 'I did ... on my own' or 'I asked for help with ...' for the child to wear home. This not only celebrates the child's successes, but also demonstrates the importance of these achievements to parents.

Engaging the reluctant

"I've tried all sorts but he never seems to want to join in."

Children may be reluctant to participate in play or adult-led activities for a variety of reasons. They may be anxious, have low self-esteem or be unfamiliar with the type of activity. These children may spend long periods of time observing others or may limit their play to a small selection of activities with which they feel comfortable.

Teaching tip

Through observation and knowledge of the child, try to establish the reasons why they do not participate. It may be a lack of understanding of the expectation, a fear of failure, avoidance of sensory experiences such as noises of a particular volume or pitch, textures or smells, maybe a need for personal space, hearing or sight problems, uncertainty about a particular child. Many sensory issues can be overcome by sensory integration programmes designed by occupational therapists.

While repeating activities can reinforce understanding and observing others is a good way to learn, children may need support to extend their play and exploration. Here are some great ideas to help children who are unable to access a varied play provision independently.

- If a child lacks confidence, engage in play near them. Do not demand their participation (or for some children even make eye contact), but model a simple action and ensure that there is sufficient space and resources for the child to join in. When the child shows an interest, gradually extend your play and only attempt to interact when the child appears comfortable.
- Once a child is involved in play, reassure them that their play is acceptable by introducing some of their ideas into your play. (If they knock their tower over then you could do the same, if they push their car off the car-mat then yours could follow). When some interaction is established, try to take a lead from the child rather than dominate the play.

- Use a child's schema. Observe any play or interests and try to include these patterns in different areas of the play provision. Common schemas, such as spinning or enclosure of objects, can be incorporated into role-play areas or sand and water play fairly easily; a role-play shop or sandpit could incorporate bags and boxes; a role-play bus, train or car will allow turning wheels, cogs or steering wheel. Once a child begins to show an interest in an area and becomes engaged you will be able to extend their play and interests.
- Initially make adult-led sessions short for the reluctant child. It is better to have a short successful session than try to extend it and have it end badly. Differentiate expectations to individual children.
- Avoid overwhelming a child with too many choices and ensure that the child is clear about the options available. It may be necessary to reduce options to a closed choice of two.
- Build up slowly. Allow children time to be alone, observe or think if that is how they gain comfort.
- Praise participation, but be aware that for a few children, receiving animated praise can be difficult. It may be that a smile and quiet well done is sufficient.

Taking it further

Discuss individual participation with all staff and monitor children of concern. Children often respond to different adults in very different ways and it may be worth changing a child's key worker to see if their engagement in activities is improved.

Involving parents

Discuss your observations of play with parents and carers and establish the types of play that are seen at home. Encourage parents to introduce new styles of play both inside and out and, if possible, to join in.

Making mistakes

"She was doing really well, but she got one wrong and then she wouldn't try any more."

Many children like to get things right first time and find it difficult to accept and learn from their mistakes. Even young children can have developed unrealistic expectations of success and will either give up or become upset when they make a mistake.

The earlier that a child can become happy about making mistakes, the more willing they will be to attempt unfamiliar activities. Use these ideas to help children to accept that initial answers will not always be correct and support them learning that mistakes are acceptable.

- Draw attention to the mistakes you make, and make it known that everyone makes mistakes.
- When a child gives an incorrect answer, praise them for having tried. 'Good try, but not quite' is much easier to accept than 'no!'
- During games and activities always praise the effort rather than the results.
- Join in with challenging activities such as building tall towers or balancing on stepping-stones. Model perseverance by restarting the task enthusiastically when you fail, and show that the apparent failure is not upsetting or off-putting.
- Provide open-ended tasks where there is no correct answer. Alongside shape inset puzzles, offer two-dimensional shapes that can be collaged or tessellated freely.
- Provide activities that encourage experimentation and include some items that will not be successful. For example in rolling activities, include cuboids or balls too large to fit down a tube. Observe children as they explore the resources and support and encourage as necessary.

Adapting behaviour

"It's fine when he runs and shouts outside, but he just carries on when he goes inside."

Children need to learn how to adapt their behaviours according to where they are. In the playground they can run shout but in an assembly hall they are expected to sit still and listen.

Use these ideas to help children recognise that spaces are used for different purposes and behaviours need to be adjusted accordingly.

- Play with a doll's house to establish that rooms in a house have different items in them and that these link with their purpose. Talk about the intention of the small world figure as they move from room to room and use different items.
- Play simple games using a doll's house or pictures of rooms. 'Where would I go to clean my teeth?' 'Where do I need to be careful because things may be hot?'
- During cooking activities or using the toilets, draw attention to safety issues and link these to the necessary behaviours.
- Introduce the idea that spaces are not always defined by walls. Play simple games with hoops or mats serving as islands. Ask children to move around the islands until a sign is given, and then to perform an action, perhaps balance on one leg/hum/shout.
- Practise using voices at different volumes. This could be incorporated into role-play for example, 'We don't want to wake the bear, we need to whisper'.
- Practise moving at different speeds. Again this could be achieved through role-play. You might be cars, animals or robots.

Teaching tip

If children are finding it difficult to slow down when moving from an outside area to inside, you could try hanging a soft bead curtain over the door. The sensation of moving through will reinforce the idea that they are moving into a different space.

Secret support

"I only have to look at him and he knows that he should stop."

Children learn to respond to physical cues and facial expression at a young age and will use these to prompt answers or actions, masking their true understanding.

We all give non-verbal messages to children, some of which are intentional, some subconscious. By becoming more aware of the messages that we are giving, we can use them to support children to learn rather than to provide answers and reduce independent thought.

- When children are required to recognise their own written name, it is natural to look at the child from whom you expect a response. Try looking away to check that it is the written word that they recognise rather than a response to your attention.
- When asking a child to count out a particular number of items into your hand, be aware that the natural instinct is to close your hand when the requested number is reached. If your hand remains open, the child may well continue to count items.
- Children will often watch your facial expression when responding to a question. They may offer a number of responses until you smile or nod. It is easy to misinterpret this, believing that the child has corrected themselves and is secure with a concept.
- Children will often select the final suggestion when offered a choice. 'Did the boat float or sink?' 'Is it wet or dry?' Try to vary the order in which the suggestions are offered.

My coat peg?

"She just throws her coat on the floor or, if we are lucky, puts it on any random peg."

Taking responsibility for their own belongings is a basic, but very necessary, skill for any child starting school.

Many children will find their coat peg with little support, but for some this will be more challenging. It is often easier and always quicker to hang the coat up yourself, but time invested in teaching a skill at this early stage will increase the child's independence both at school and home.

- Clearly written name labels can be accompanied by a simple, appealing picture. For children who are struggling to find their peg, ask parents about their child's interests and link the picture to this.
- Some children find visual processing difficult and may not respond to two-dimensional images. For these children a small, familiar toy could be hung on the peg.
- Mount peg labels on different coloured papers, find out if an individual child has a preference for a certain colour.
- A peg at the end of a row is easier for a child who is struggling to identify their peg.
- Anticipate the problem. Be ready to support the child as soon as they arrive at your setting. It is easier to encourage a child to hang their coat up than to have to find them so they can pick it up off the floor.

Teaching tip

For a short time, while you are trying to establish the behaviour, give an incentive to the child for finding their peg. This could be a sticker that could be collected there, or a favourite toy hung there. Persevere. It may take weeks!

Taking it further

Once the child has learnt to recognise their coat peg, identical labelling can be used for their wellies, their drink bottle and their work file.

It's mine!

"Putting the go-kart out always causes arguments. It's always the same children who get a turn."

Sharing is always difficult for young children and issues around turn-taking can spark arguments and resentment.

Children will have very different experiences of sharing at home and many will need to be taught to take turns with their peers. Intervention and modelling can help children to learn to share and take turns independently.

- When observing children, watch for physical pushing, snatching, hoarding and carrying toys, hiding favourite toys, use of adults to win toys, verbal assertiveness or intimidation.
- Model turn-taking through adult-led games that focus on short turns and the handing of resources or toys from child to child. These could take the form of a simple board game, passing a dice, or simple relay races.
- Verbalise turn-taking, drawing attention to the fact that children are taking turns successfully, for example 'it's Ben's turn now'.
- When a child finds it difficult to pass on a favourite toy, give a clear minute warning 'one more minute then it's Jade's turn'. When the minute is up, ensure that the child not only hands the toy on, but is happy. You may need to distract them with another toy or reassure them that it will be their turn again soon.
- We all encourage children to speak to adults to resolve difficulties, but be aware that some children will overuse this and will gain toys from others unfairly.
- Draw attention to good and poor sharing as it arises in picture books and discuss how the characters may feel about this.
- Try to make sharing fun, not a punishment.

Do I get a turn?

"I'm sure she wants a turn, but she just stands back and waits."

It is always easier to spot those children who dominate the toys, refusing to share. Children who are reluctant to assert themselves need support to learn techniques that will allow them to push themselves forward and take their turn.

Children who stand back may lack confidence; be wary of the response of certain children; be unfamiliar with the concept of turn-taking; struggle to maintain concentration on the structure of turn-taking or be too polite to push themselves forward in a crowd.

- Introduce the use of large sand timers by fixed equipment such as swings. Teach children to use the timers independently and monitor from a distance. It is important that a child who operates the timer is successful in establishing a turn. Timers reduce the need for language and are seen to be fair.
- Introduce symbols such as a photo of the object to be shared, which can be held, to indicate that a child is waiting. This establishes an order for turn-taking.
- Occasionally, ask a more assertive child, who is also waiting, to support a less confident child to establish a turn. 'Nathan's turn is before yours Ben', Ben will be keen to get Nathan to take his turn!
- Ensure that simple turn-taking is understood through modelling and adult-led, structured play sessions.
- Encourage the child to ask for adult support. Initially support the child fully, modelling necessary behaviours, and then gradually reduce support.
- Praise any progress.

Teaching tip

When working in groups, it can sometimes be beneficial to group less confident children together, allowing them to establish a turn without the competition from their more assertive peers.

Taking it further

Observation of behaviour is vital in supporting a child who struggles to assert themselves with their peers. Identification of the problem is often more difficult than resolving it.

13

The basics

Part 2

Learning to learn

"He spent ages building a bridge with the Duplo but when I asked him to work with me he was ready to leave after a couple of minutes."

Children are more likely to persevere to find successful strategies when engaged in self-chosen and self-directed activities. Given time, appropriately stimulating opportunities and sensitive adult support, children will begin to organise their thoughts.

Teaching tip

Allow children sufficient time to work in a gentle and unhurried way. Children may repeat actions several times to secure and test their own understanding.

The following ideas aim to help adults support children's reflections on their own learning and their ability to connect areas of existing knowledge. The role of the adult in these situations is to encourage and prompt, not to provide answers or information.

- Provide a wide variety of opportunities for investigation both inside and out. Ensure that resources are stimulating and the activities are not competitive. Activities may include almost anything, including construction materials, magnifying glasses, story-telling props etc.
- Observe the child's exploration. Try to identify their interests and dilemmas.
- Prompt further thinking by joining the child in their investigation. Take care not to tell children how to solve problems but question to encourage perseverance and imagination.
- Use open questioning to ask how they have achieved their aims. This will focus their attention on the process involved in their investigation.
- When situations arise, model the learning process by involving children in your own dilemmas. For example, when asked a question you could reply 'I'm not sure. I wonder how I could find out. Maybe I should...' or 'I need to think about that.'

Taking it further

Help children to become aware of their own learning path by asking questions such as 'what did you need to do?', 'how did you manage to do that?' or 'what helped you to...?' Children my need support to answer initially but will benefit from modelling.

16

Day to day routines

"She always likes to sit in the same place at fruit time. She got really upset when Jamie sat there."

Children like and need routines as they provide security and stability. Familiar routines within an Early Years setting allow transitions between activities to flow smoothly. Children will learn to anticipate what will happen soon and understand that something will end in order for another activity to begin.

While establishing routines is important, it is equally important to help children to appreciate that routines are not set in stone and will sometimes change. Some children will accept these changes without question, others, especially those on the autistic spectrum, may become anxious or cross. The ideas that follow may help children who struggle to understand routines or resist change.

- Verbalise routines as they occur; for example '... has finished. It's time for...'.
- Simplify routines to now and next. 'We are going to tidy up now and go outside to play next' or for children whose language is less developed, 'Tidy up now, outside to play next'.
- Use simple visual timetables with clear pictorial representations of activities. Refer to these when initiating a change of activity. These make the structure of the day clear without the need for complex language.
- When changes in routine occur, don't try to hide them. Describe the change and, if appropriate, explain the reasons for this and replace the image on the visual timetable. Some children respond well to an Oops Card to represent a change in routine.
- For children who find it difficult to leave an activity, give a one-minute warning before the change.

Teaching tip

Look out for self-established routines such as lining up toy cars or repeating behaviour. These may provide the child with security but are not sustainable in the long term. Try to distract the child from these behaviours and discuss any concerns with your SENCO.

Exploratory play

"He just waits for me to tell him what to do when we try something new."

Children need to have the freedom to explore resources in order to test ideas and develop their understanding. The majority of children approach exploratory play with a natural curiosity and interest; some children, however, require more support.

Try these ideas to help your children engage in hands-on exploratory play activities.

- Provide a variety of open-ended activities each day. These could include large-scale planks and blocks for children to build into bridges and ramps for physical play, free collage, and colour mixing or play dough with a wide variety of tools.
- Encourage children to participate by demonstrating exploratory play possibilities, clearly indicating enjoyment and surprise. You might dig in soil and call children to watch a worm wiggle, or you may collect cars, balls and cardboard tubes to roll down a slope that you have built.
- Allow hesitant children to copy your play initially, but watch for any deviations from this. Show an interest in their ideas, however small, and extend their exploration by asking simple open-ended questions like 'what will you do now?'
- Allow children time to explore and reinforce their understanding. It may seem dull to an adult to repeat an activity over and over, but children need to repeat actions in order to learn that the result is the same. A ball will always roll down; water will always spill when poured into a full container.
- Be aware of any sensory processing issues. Some children will not want to touch certain textures or tolerate loud sounds or strong smells.

Helping or hindering experimental play?

"I know that the children should be allowed to explore independently, so what do I do?"

It is important that children are in control of their exploratory play. They learn to make decisions and choices, take on roles, negotiate with others, apply their skills and devise and solve problems. However adults have an important role to play.

The role of the adult is to support exploratory play and learning rather than direct it, allowing children to lead their own learning.

- Begin by observing the independent play.
- If play has become repetitive or stuck, join the play, ensuring that role allocation or activity is decided by the children. Ask open questions to prompt a change from the repetition.
- If children are finding it difficult to agree, join the play and support the negotiations. Be careful not to dictate the decisions but make the opinions clear and highlight the need for a solution. 'So, Ahmed wants to use this spade and so do you. You can't both use it at the same time so what could you do?'
- Use your role in the play to introduce and reinforce language. Differentiate this to suit the children involved and use it only as part of the play, don't force it!
- Model desirable behaviour and responses. Show an interest in the discoveries that the children make.
- Sometimes it is best to stand back from successful play situations and use the opportunity to make detailed observations and gain a greater understanding of a child's learning styles and levels of development. Use this knowledge to inform your planning.

Teaching tip

It can be difficult to differentiate between a child who is repeating an action to test and secure an understanding and a child who is displaying repetitive, stuck play. Look for the child's engagement, interest and response to the result of their own actions. You could ask them to show you what they are doing.

Observing for planning

"She was trying to build the small bricks into Jack's beanstalk but she couldn't get them to balance. She was so pleased when I got the big bricks out and even put a little one on the top!"

Perceptive observations provide invaluable evidence about a child's interests and their ability to apply existing skills and understanding to different situations.

The following ideas help adults to use their observations of children during self-directed play to inform their planning for play provision. This type of formative assessment can also influence the immediate adult support given.

- Look at the way in which children are using the resources. Can they use them independently? Are there changes that could be made to support or extend the play? If a child is dressing a doll, is there a variety of different clothes available? Is the child able to manage the fastenings or do they give up because they are too difficult?
- Look at the knowledge that is being used in play. Do they use number names in order or match similar objects? Which resources could be provided to encourage further practice?
- Are jigsaw puzzles too easy or difficult? Are the images appealing to the children?
- Are children using items to represent other items in role-play? For example, are beads being used as money? Consider placing small items such as bricks or shapes near role-play areas. Children may use them as food, money, medicine, telephones etc. using their imagination and own ideas in their play.
- If a child always chooses to play with a particular toy, try placing these toys in different situations, inside or outside, to use their interests as a means to extend their play experiences.

Involving parents

Encourage parents and carers to share their own observations made at home. These will help to build a picture of the child's learning.

Getting dressed

"Blessen doesn't even try to get changed. He waits for us to do it for him."

Some children learn to get themselves dressed at an early age, others struggle. At school, children will be expected to change for PE and swimming quickly and independently, taking responsibility for their own clothes.

In order to prepare children for school, it is valuable to introduce some activities that involve taking off and putting on items of clothing. Some of the following ideas may reduce the frustration of lost socks and half-dressed children running off to play!

- Children find sequencing clothes difficult and will often put on their sweatshirt only to find that they are left with a T-shirt. Place clothes in a pile so that children can work from the top. Some children will be able to respond to symbol cards, indicating an order in which to work.
- Wherever possible, try not to correct early independent attempts at self-dressing. Encourage parents to celebrate their child's achievement rather than criticise them for putting a T-shirt on back-to-front.
- Plan role-play areas to include dressing-up and clothes for dolls and teddies with fastenings such as buttons and zips. Encourage children to persevere with these through play.
- If clothes are constantly being mixed up or lost, give children a named box.
- In order to give a child a sense of success, backward chain the task, allowing the child to complete the dressing independently. Gradually reduce the support offered, always encouraging independence to finish.

Involving parents

Encourage parents and carers to dress children in clothes that are easy to take on and off. Avoid belts, buckles and laces and ensure that tops are large enough to wiggle out of easily. Acknowledge that it is time-consuming, but ask parents to support their child to dress as independently as possible.

Behaving badly

"He always pushes the other children and just carries on when I tell him to stop. He seems to enjoy being told off!"

All children misbehave occasionally and most respond to a gentle reprimand. Some children repeat their poor behaviour patterns and need a more structured approach to behaviour management.

The following ideas can be used to develop a behaviour plan for an individual who misbehaves repeatedly.

- Young children may be misbehaving to gain attention. They may enjoy the animated expressions on the cross adult face. Wherever possible, give little animated response to poor behaviour.
- Discuss consequences of poor behaviour with your team. Many settings use a short time out in which a child sits away from the group for a short time. If time out is used, do not talk to the child during this time as you will be giving attention to and reinforcing the cycle of bad behaviour.
- Whatever the consequence of poor behaviour, it needs to be short. When the child returns to the group, state the desired behaviour, for example 'be kind to your friends' rather than the negative 'don't hit'.
- Avoid discussing a child's behaviour in front of them.
- If a child is finding it difficult to maintain good behaviour, try to give them attention as soon as you spot any positive play. This gives the message that good behaviour gains attention that is fun, while poor behaviour results in little attention and a boring time.

Learn it here, use it there

"He can count when we sit at the table and I put the blocks in a line, but he hasn't got a clue when he's anywhere else."

When children learn a new skill they need to practise and test it in many different contexts in order to secure their understanding.

Transferring knowledge from one situation to another can be difficult. Children often begin to gain an understanding of a concept or skill by observing others, copying, or learning by rote. Providing a stimulating play environment and sensitive support can encourage children to generalise their learning.

- When planning your play provision, ensure that different areas of learning are addressed in different contexts each week. For example, one week numbers may be hidden in sand, the next, written in chalk on a wall as part of a ball game, the next, in number jigsaw puzzles.
- Discuss any emerging skills with all staff and provide any necessary support or modelling to develop individual progress. Observe self-directed play to identify secure understanding.
- Plan based on topics then allow children to explore using play opportunities. The idea of floating and sinking in water could be introduced through a story about a boat and explored through indoor water play with different items, some of which float and some sink. Clear lidded bottles part-filled with water and a mixture of small items (for example buttons, washers, polystyrene balls etc.) allow children to recognise that the metal washer always sinks while the plastic brick will always float.

Involving parents

Keep parents and carers informed of any emerging skills. Suggest contexts in which these skills can be modelled and practised. For example, if a child is beginning to recognise the repeat in a pattern, this could be explored at home by finding repeats in tiles, packaging or perhaps arranging fruit or cakes on a plate.

Feeling happy?

"He doesn't seem to notice when he hurts someone."

The development of an understanding of emotions is extremely complex but there are many simple ideas that can support a child to recognise and respond appropriately to basic facial expressions and emotions.

Taking it further

The majority of children will make significant progress in their understanding of emotions during their pre-school age years. However, some children, especially those on the autistic spectrum, will struggle. Discuss concerns with the child's parents and your SENCO. Early identification and action can make a difference.

Very young children often love to watch an animated face and may mirror the expressions they see. The ideas below draw links between facial expressions and familiar feelings, linking these to a child's own experiences.

- When a child is showing a clear emotion, verbalise the reasons for that feeling. Just a simple sentence will do; 'oh dear, you have hurt your knee and now you're feeling sad. I'm going to help you to feel better'.
- When reading stories, name the emotions felt by characters and discuss the reasons that they feel the way they do.
- Show children photos and symbols showing basic emotions. Draw attention to the significant differences between them. Use these cards when reading stories.
- Play simple sorting games, placing pictures of events into 'makes me happy' or 'makes me sad' piles. More complex emotions can be used with more able children.
- Praise and reward children for showing concern or helping others who are upset.
- Acknowledge that it is OK to feel sad or cross sometimes.
- Work one to one with a child who becomes aggressive when angry. Recognise that anger is a normal emotion and suggest alternative responses. Physical activity, squeezing a cushion or moving to a safe area may help. Draw attention to the effect of the child's actions on others.

You go and get it!

"I can't be bothered to do sticking. There's too much waiting."

A child who struggles to locate and use the resources necessary for an activity may well avoid trying. These ideas will help children to develop independence when selecting, collecting and using resources.

Allowing independent access to resources may create more mess initially but the opportunities for learning are worth a bit of clearing up!

- Whenever possible, taking into account safety issues, have basic resources available for children to access independently at all times. Try to keep their location consistent.
- Encourage creativity indoors by providing a free space near the papers, glues and mark making tools to allow free exploration.
- While glue sticks are less messy, also provide and teach children to use PVA glue with a spreader as well. PVA sticks work best when only a thin layer is applied and the two-handed activity of wiping the excess glue off the spreader onto the side of the pot is brilliant for developing fine motor skills.
- While basic resources may always be available, add new ones for short periods. Toothbrushes and cotton wool buds can be used in paint and sand trays, and lolly sticks and cotton reels are fun in play dough. Decorating brushes and sponges dipped in water are great for making large marks on bare walls. The possibilities are endless!

Teaching tip

Observe whether individual children know how to use glue, scissors, play dough etc. It can take many attempts and demonstrations for a child to remember that the glue-covered surface has to be placed downwards in order for it to stick!

Bonus idea

Encourage children to select and use their own natural resources when working outside. Sticks and leaves make interesting marks when dragged through paint.

Making instructions clear

"He ignores what I say and just copies the other children."

Children's understanding of the spoken word develops at different rates. A lack of comprehension may be an indication of a language difficulty or delay but could equally be due to a lack of experience.

Teaching tip

If difficulties in understanding persist, you should discuss these with your SENCO who may need to speak to parents and involve speech therapists. Early intervention can often prevent many problems later.

Children need to develop the skills involved in understanding and responding to instructions. A child who is told, 'get your jacket and go outside' may not know that jacket means 'coat'; they may not know where their jacket is, or even where outside is.

- Do not assume that the child's lack of response to instructions is defiance. Repeating the instruction in a cross voice generally doesn't work!
- Use body language and gesture to support instructions; over 50% of messages are conveyed non-verbally.
- Ensure that the child can see and hear you before giving instructions.
- If the child fails to respond to a complex sentence, reduce the number of words used, focussing on those that carry the information. For example, 'now you need to cut around the edges of the chicken shape before you start gluing' may become 'cutting now' supported with pointing.
- Model the use of key words during an activity, to help a child make links between the language and the task.
- Experiment with instructions in a variety of situations; the child may struggle to filter out the sounds of a noisy Early Years environment to focus on your words.
- Praise even small successes using simple language and smiles. This will encourage the child to make the effort again.

Exploring the senses

Part 3

Look and see

"He will turn his head but doesn't show much interest in the things he can see."

Early Years settings are usually bright and colourful places. While children often respond to visually stimulating displays and activities, they can equally become distracted or overwhelmed.

Activities in which individuals have some control over the colour or light and shade can help children to develop visual processing skills. The following ideas are designed to use visual contrast or detail to engage the interest of young children and to encourage them to use their sense of sight to find out about the world around them.

- Contrasting colours can draw attention to displays. Opposite colours are red and green, blue and orange, yellow and purple. Displays that are only black, white and grey can be equally striking.
- Add silver foil or plastic mirrors to add a reflective surface to collages, or three-dimensional work. Silver foil stretched over a table can completely change the way in which children will play with a construction toy.
- Light boxes can be used to explore colour, light and shade. Try getting the same effect using sweet wrappers stretched over torches.
- Make dark spaces in large cardboard boxes and tunnels. You can hide objects inside and encourage children to find them with or without a torch.
- Encourage children to look for detail, hide small items in the sand tray or ask them to follow a fine red thread around an outside area.

Bonus idea ★

Treasure hunts using photographs of small parts of fixed objects, such as a close-up of the handle on a shed or a step of a slide, can encourage children to look at items in a different way. They will need to look for details and use clues of colour, shape and texture.

Smashing smells!

"She loves to smell the soap and always sniffs my jumper. It's amazing; she can tell whose sweatshirt it is by smelling it!"

Smell is often the sense that is thought to be the least important and can be over-looked in a busy Early Years environment. Introducing activities in which smell is a factor can generate a surprising interest among young children.

While some of the following ideas are possible at any time of the year, others lend themselves more readily to different seasons and can highlight changes in the natural world. Activities that stimulate sensory awareness can support scientific enquiry and exploration.

- Make rose petal perfume. Adding water and mashing most flower petals will increase their smell and children will love grinding them using a pestle and mortar or wooden spoon in a bowl. You can do the same with herbs to explore their smells.
- Add vanilla, peppermint, lemon or orange food extracts to the water tray, play dough, paint or collage materials.
- Plant herbs in a sensory garden or window box. Encourage children to squeeze or rub the leaves before smelling them.
- Encourage children to match smells. Place small amounts of items with a strong smell into pots with fabric stretched over the top. Items may include cotton wool soaked in food extracts, lavender, pot pourri, soap, crushed mint leaves, spices etc. Make two or more pots of each smell and offer only a small selection each time.
- Draw attention to the smell of different ingredients during cooking activities.

Teaching tip

If children are willing, try blindfolding them when smelling different items. It may stop them trying to cheat when matching! Sleep masks from planes are ideal as they are easy to put on and remove and do not need to be too tight.

Sounds good!

"He makes noises all the time, either clicking his tongue, humming or tapping things."

Most Early Years settings have a selection of musical instruments that are available to children to have a go with and many have song time. Children often love to explore sounds and these activities can also promote collaboration.

It can be difficult in a busy Early Years setting to allow free exploration of sound making resources without distracting other children and annoying adults. Working outdoors can help or you could timetable short noisy sessions before a song time.

- When making shakers, encourage children to experiment with containers and contents. Containers may be cardboard boxes, tins, plastic pots or tubes with paper, foil or cellophane stretched over the end. Items to put inside may include rice, pasta, small stones or metal nuts and bolts. Close supervision will be needed to make sure small items are not misused!
- Try making sounds using natural materials collected on a walk or brought in from home.
- Children may be able to make sounds by blowing across the tops of bottles.
- Simple kazoo-type instruments can be made by stretching elastic bands over two lolly sticks before sandwiching short lengths of drinking straws between them. The sound is made by humming into them and varies according to straw length. These are best made shortly before home time!

Taking it further

Encourage children to play instruments together, in time to a rhythm or to accompany a familiar song. Working together you can introduce the concept of loud and soft, high and low or a fast and slow beat.

Touch and feel

"She spends ages washing her hands, I think she just likes the feel of it."

Sensory seekers can find the stimulation gained from texture pleasurable and even calming, while others may find the same experience to be too much.

Introducing and encouraging children to use touch appropriately when exploring their environment can help them to learn to process the stimulation that their body receives and to develop a sense of curiosity.

- When planning cooking activities, include those that require rubbing in, such as making scones or shortbread. Model the action and talk about the texture of the flour and butter.
- Encourage children to use their hands when mark making with paint. Handprints are the obvious activity, but fingers can be used to drag paint across a surface. Try varying the surface; paint dragged across a plastic surface feels very different from finger painting on paper or card.
- Include texture play in your continuous provision. Cornflour mixed with water feels dry but dribbles through fingers. Add rice or lentils to play dough to provide a different texture. Provide both wet and dry sand side by side. There are a number of thickeners for water that make a texture similar to wallpaper paste that can be used in the water tray.
- Consider texture when collecting items for collage. Ensure that the adult supporting the activity is prepared to join in and show enjoyment with texture play.
- If children avoid the activities described above, work slowly. Start by encouraging a child to use one finger and build up. Praise participation.

Teaching tip

Plan for messy, sticky children! Talk about how much fun it can be to get mucky at times but also point out the problems that this can cause. Show children where they can wash their hands nearby to avoid a trail of sticky marks along walls.

Bonus idea ★

Don't stop with hands! Children will often love to feel with their feet. Walking on fur or through paint can produce a lot of giggles.

Tastes good!

"He loves to lick the glue sticks and always puts the play dough in his mouth."

Putting objects in their mouths may be a comforting habit for young children or they may be seeking the sensory stimulation from the taste, texture or temperature on the lips and mouth.

Many of the activities below provide a perfect opportunity to teach children about hygiene, healthy eating and safety issues. The promise of sampling flavours will encourage many children to follow hand-washing routines and engage in the activity. Children need to be taught when it is safe and appropriate to taste items but many will find activities that involve taste to be motivating.

- Introduce food-tasting sessions; these could link to books, topics on countries, fruit and vegetables, a particular colour or festival.
- Encourage children to express their likes and dislikes.
- Some children may be prepared to be blindfolded for blind tasting. If children aren't keen, volunteer a staff member and allow children to watch their response and listen to their comments.
- Try to provide contrasting flavours and always end with a favourite!
- Explore different textures such as rice crispies, breadsticks, raisins, orange segments, ice-lollies etc.
- Encourage children to taste before they make choices of pizza topping or sandwich fillings etc.

See, feel, smell, hear, play

"There's one child who still carries a comfort blanket. He spends ages just sniffing it and rubbing it on his upper lip."

A multisensory approach that encourages children to use their senses appropriately to explore their world can help to engage and develop an enquiring mind.

Giving a little thought and making a few changes to the sensory experiences that are provided in an Early Years continuous play provision can help to engage and interest young children and provide variety and choice.

- Home made play dough can be easily adapted. Add rice or beads to vary the texture; food colouring or paint to vary colour, glitter to add sparkle, or peppermint, lemon or vanilla essence to alter the smell.
- When creating an interactive display, consider using different cloths to cover the table; artificial fur, wax cloth, felt, netting etc.
- Use a wide variety of textures in collage and three-dimensional work. Including reflective materials such as tin foil on a robot can add visual and textural interest.
- You can also create a collage to smell using herbs, spices and flowers. Encourage children to make considered choices, using their senses to find out about the items before selecting.
- Add food extracts and colouring to the water tray, or vary the temperature. Children will love to play with toy penguins in a water tray with ice floating in it. Pick your day for this, if it is too cold then children will get extremely cold, and if it is too hot then you will need to replenish the ice too frequently!
- Rice crispies in a tray feel and sound fantastic as they are crushed. Children may even taste them!

Teaching tip

As a prompt to include multisensory opportunities in your play provision, why not add a checklist of senses to tick on your planning sheet.

Bonus idea

Ask children to bring in items to put in 'sensory boxes'. A 'feely box' could focus on a particular texture each week, while a 'noise box' could contain objects that make different sounds. You could even have 'smell boxes' as well!

Too loud!

"Whenever there's a loud noise, he puts his hands over his ears and gets cross."

Many children find it difficult to process sound and some have a negative response to sounds that other children would hardly notice.

Some children with special needs may find loud sounds particularly distressing and they may limit the activities that they will want to join in with. These children may benefit from wearing headphones or ear-defenders to soften the sound.

These activities improve auditory discrimination and help children to recognise where sounds are coming from and identify those that can be ignored and those that require their attention. Anxiety and stress should reduce as an understanding of sound develops.

- Watch out for signs that a child is struggling to process sound. They may put their hands over their ears; struggle to block out background noises and become distracted by these; require instructions to be repeated; become tearful, violent, irritable or withdrawn.
- Practise identifying the sound source and direction by playing circle sound games in which one child sits in the centre of a circle with their eyes closed. A child in the circle plays an instrument sound and the child in the centre tries to point to the direction of the sound and identify the instrument.
- Listen to sounds in the environment and try to identify them.
- Draw attention to the rhythms of the spoken word through clapping the rhythms of names, words or nursery rhymes.
- Encourage focussed listening by occasionally whispering. The whisper must be motivating, for example 'shall we see what is in the box?' and should be in a quiet area.
- Play listening bingo games; ask children to focus on the given sound and identify what would usually produce it.

Involving parents

Parents may find it useful to introduce quiet times at home when televisions and computers are turned off and a child is able to focus on a quiet conversation or game.

Learning to move

Part 4

Strong fingers

"I get him to hold a pencil but he presses so lightly it hardly makes a mark."

As children develop their fine motor skills, they will need to use their fingers in a variety of ways that will depend upon the strength and dexterity of their hands and fingers. Help children to develop strength and coordination to facilitate the mechanics of writing, drawing and tool manipulation.

Involving parents

Share these ideas with parents so they repeat them with their children at home. The more practice children have, the more skilled they will become.

Children need to develop the strength to hold and grip with all fingers working together as well as the ability to isolate individual fingers to perform individual actions. Here are some short, fun activities that can be adapted to fit in with a variety of topics.

- The action of opening and closing scissors can be practised by using glove puppets that open and close their mouths.
- Finger and thumb strength, necessary to maintain a pencil grip, can be improved by clipping clothes pegs onto a card. The card can be shaped so that the pegs become the legs of a caterpillar or the whiskers of a cat. Increase the pressure required to squeeze thumb and fingers together by using bulldog clips or freezer-bag clips.
- Encourage children to shape dough or clay by squeezing and pinching with their fingers. You could make flower petals by pinching small pieces of clay and by squeezing their bases together you could form flowers.
- Make collages by screwing up small balls of coloured tissue paper using fingertips.
- Use round ended or plastic scissors to snip dough and make hedgehogs!
- Encourage children to pick up small items using large plastic tweezers.
- Pop bubble wrap using fingers only. It will be tricky to resist a satisfying squeeze!

Bonus idea ★

Try stretching cling film over a plastic pot. Encourage children to pierce the film using the point of a pencil to increase the pressure and strength of their grip.

This hand, that hand

"It's funny. He uses his left hand to draw on the paper on his left side, then swaps to his right for that side."

Children may swap hands half way across their body when mark making or using basic tools. This does not mean that the child is ambidextrous, however, and can make tasks more difficult.

There are a variety of activities that can be easily included in an Early Years setting which will help children to cross their midline, using one hand to complete a task. These activities can help to develop hand-eye coordination and motor planning, both necessary for drawing and writing, but they are not designed to force a hand dominance.

- A kneeling position reduces the whole body movement and encourages the use of a full arm movement. Children who are unable to kneel can be supported at their hips (with cushions on chairs with sides for example), to achieve a similar stability.
- Encourage the child to high kneel in front of a board and draw a rainbow making large arched lines from one side of the board to the other.
- Place a peg board to the right of a child and a pot of pegs on the left. Encourage the child to pick up pegs and place them in the board without swapping hands. Swap the positions of the board and pegs and repeat.
- Support a child to high kneel or sit securely to move cotton reels along a rope or beads on an abacus from one side to the other.
- Work on hands and knees, pushing a car or train from one side of their body to the other. They will need the support of one arm and so will be forced to cross their midline in their movement.

Teaching tip

Use circle activities in which objects are passed around from one child to the next to practise the skills involved in crossing the midline. Ask children to use one hand only. You can swap hands and direction.

Bonus idea ★

Sing 'Head, Shoulders Knees and Toes', insisting that both knees, shoulders, ears etc. are touched but only using one hand. Children may get in a muddle but this can be fun!

37

Drawing with direction

"The pencil just goes where it wants."

There are several skills that need to be developed before children are able to use a pencil with reasonable control. If some of these are established before attempts are made to write, children will progress more quickly and become less frustrated.

Children who find pencil control difficult may benefit from a wide variety of activities that develop their strength, spatial awareness and motor planning. Include some of the activities below; children will have fun and will not know that they are preparing for handwriting!

- Weight bearing activities that focus on shoulders and hips such as crawling and monkey bars help develop strength.
- Pushing and pulling trolleys, wheelbarrows or bikes can develop strength but can also allow exploration of distance and direction. Set up simple chalk roads or paths that wiggle to challenge children.
- Encourage children to follow lines or tracks with their hands and fingers. Including textures on these tracks can add motivation and give sensory feedback to the child. Pushing a train along a track, anticipating bends and maintaining a hold on the train is a good way to practise these skills.
- Allow lots of time and opportunities for free mark making with different tools.
- Help children to develop horizontal and vertical scribbling by holding two strips of wood on the paper, forming a curbed gap between them. Create a wide gap, and reduce the space as the child bumps into the sides less.
- Make a task clear and fun. Avoid trying to form letters too early. Children may enjoy drawing lines from one point to another on a treasure island or making a river in the sand tray.

Simple tools

"I always put the same play dough tools out because I know they can't hurt themselves with them."

Many tasks in Early Years settings involve the use of basic tools, with the objective being to master the use of the tool itself. In a Key Stage One classroom, the efficient use of the tool allows the child to focus on different learning objectives.

It is important that all children are taught to use glue spreaders, shaping tools and mark making implements as independently and accurately as possible.

- Children need to be taught that tools have a purpose. When introducing a tool take time to look at the component parts and link these to their purpose. Demonstrate their use and supervise early exploration. A child who turns all items into a weapon may not be quite sure of an item's intended use.
- Model the efficient way to hold tools. Sometimes it is easier to handle and use tools standing rather than sitting. More pressure can be applied and a clearer view gained.
- We often encourage the imaginative use of items to represent others in role-play. Children need to learn that this is not always appropriate or safe. Teach children to respect tools.
- Silhouettes of tool shapes on shelves remind children to put tools away and also serve as a quick visual check that all tools have been returned.
- Name tools accurately from the start. More able children can extend their language skills when asked to describe how to use a tool, while the less able may be able to select, for example, a spoon to stir in a cookery session.

Teaching tip

Allow time for children to practise using tools and provide a variety of contexts for exploration. A play dough shaping tool could also be used in wet sand or maybe even paint.

Taking it further

When children have been introduced to a variety of tools, try to plan activities that allow a choice of tools. Talk to children about the choices that they make.

Scissor skills

"It is scary watching him with scissors, he doesn't look at where he is cutting and the scissors seem to slip out of his hand."

Children who are able to use scissors independently and accurately are able to approach many tasks at school with confidence. The fine motor skills and visual focus that is needed is necessary in a range of tasks.

Cutting around shapes is rarely the focus of a school activity but can be vital in order to complete a task neatly. Many children struggle to coordinate their two hands simultaneously, to control the scissors and the paper when cutting.

- The action of opening and closing scissors can be practised with sprung scissors that only require pressure to close.
- For early cutting tasks, provide thin card, which will cut more easily without bending.
- Ensure that scissors are fit for purpose. Many children's scissors cut badly.
- Initially focus on random short cuts from the edge of the shape, for example creating the mane of a lion.
- Next, draw short lines from the edge of the paper. Encourage the child to hold the paper and position the scissors before squeezing to cut.
- Once children can control the position of a short snip, draw widely spaced parallel lines. These should be straight to begin and gradually bend and curve as skills increase. First ask the child to point along the track, starting from the edge nearest to their body. Next, guide their hand as they make the snipping action with scissors in a practise run. Finally ask them to attempt to cut between the lines.
- When introducing the idea of cutting around a shape, draw an entry line from the edge of the page.

Taking it further

More able children can extend their skills by cutting more complex shapes that include zigzags and wavy lines as well as attempting to cut paper and card of different thicknesses. Always be aware of the safety implications when giving more challenging tasks.

Space for me

"He often forgets to duck down when he goes through the tunnel and so he bumps his head."

For some children, spatial awareness can develop slowly which may result in poor coordination skills. Using other children and objects to define the spaces around them could lead to them struggling to understand the social requirement for personal space.

Children can learn and practise skills that improve their spatial awareness through experimenting and repeating movements that require spatial judgement and give sensory feedback.

- Clapping and finger movement games and songs such as 'Two Little Dicky Birds' will help children to plan movements for their own hands and fingers.
- Encourage children to push cars along a pre-drawn track. The direction of the track will dictate the movement and should be varied, including twists and bends in the road.
- Jigsaws/inset puzzles and construction toys require judgements to be made about position and orientation of pieces.
- Play games with balloons; try hitting them into the air with hands or bats. Children may need quite a lot of space, as they will find it hard to hit the balloons and not other children!
- Roll balls along a drawn track or at a target.
- Jump over puddles or in and out of hoops, making judgements about the distance needed to travel.
- Make obstacle courses in which children travel over, under or through furniture, boxes or play equipment. Support children by talking about the necessary movements, for example 'don't forget to lift your feet'.

Teaching tip

Children who have impaired vision in one eye (or wear an eye patch) will struggle to judge distance accurately. Guide them with movements several times before encouraging them to attempt it independently.

41

Speaking and listening

Part 5

Listen to me

"I wish he would just listen!"

Some children will arrive at your setting able to listen well, and others will show little interest in what you say.

Taking it further

There are many games that encourage listening such as farm sound bingo games. These are a good way to motivate children to listen. You could suggest that parents play similar games at home.

A lack of response to the spoken word could be an indication of a hearing difficulty or a learning or language delay but could equally be that a child is more interested in other activities in the environment. Monitor the child's response to listening activities and raise any ongoing concerns with the SENCO and the child's parents.

- Children will be motivated to listen by fun! Make sure all activities are short and enjoyable.
- You will often hear about the importance of eye contact. Some children find this extremely difficult and uncomfortable and insistence on this during an activity may make progress slow.
- Play simple 'Simon Says' style games, initially supporting understanding by joining in with the actions and then waiting for the child to initiate the movement. Provide extra challenges to more able children by asking them to follow a verbal instruction while you perform a different one.
- Allow the child time to process the language, by leaving several seconds before you repeat or simplify the request.
- Be aware of the non-verbal clues that you are providing, such as eye pointing or hand movements.

Listen to us

"She never seems to hear what the other children say."

Increasingly, children are encouraged to discuss ideas with their peers. Children need to be able to listen within a group situation in order to benefit from this peer learning.

Listening to other members of a group and transferring attention from one speaker to another can be difficult for many children. They need to learn to focus their attention on the speaker and ignore the background noise and movement from other people.

- If possible, use areas that are quieter for group work, with fewer distractions. Furniture or screens can be used to separate a space.
- Short circle activities allow children to see each member of the group as they speak. In turn-taking, while it is good to allow children to anticipate their turn by working around the circle, it can also be beneficial to move in a more random way, encouraging children to attend to different children.
- Photos of the children in the group drawn from a bag by one child to hand to the child in the photo will help to encourage scanning and focussing skills. When the activity is established it can easily be extended by adding an action or asking a question as the photo is handed on.
- Play simple sound games in which children need to locate an item that makes a noise. The noisy item can be hidden in the room for many to try to find or behind an individual child seated in a circle.
- During a story session, vary the volume and pitch of your voice and encourage children to mimic this. This activity demands a greater attention on the listening itself and does not rely on an understanding of vocabulary.

Teaching tip

Always be aware of children who have a temporary or permanent hearing difficulty. Ensure that they have a clear line of vision to the speaker and seek advice if you are concerned.

Talk to me

"Most of the time I just have to guess what she is saying."

Children develop speech at different rates. Early support can develop communication skills, but also impact on a child's confidence within a group.

Children of all abilities benefit from adult modelling of communication skills and opportunities to extend their vocabulary in a meaningful context. Initial one to one support does not necessarily involve withdrawal from the group. These ideas for short, incidental interactions during play can help to develop functional language.

- Repeat words and phrases back to children as a way to confirm understanding and to model correct pronunciation and word order. Do not force the child to repeat their comment correctly. They may avoid talking to you again if they feel criticised!
- Use context clues and gesture to establish an understanding.
- Don't pretend to have understood a child; some children will give up if they are constantly misunderstood.
- Make it clear that you are interested in what the child has to say.
- Play simple naming games where the word to be said is known. Model and repeat words. This type of activity will help you tune in to a child's speech patterns, helping you to understand them in different contexts.
- Play nonsense sound repeating games, for example 'My Turn, Your Turn'. These will help establish the turn-taking nature of conversation but also help to develop an ability to form a variety of sounds without the fear of failure. Ensure that you face the child so that they can see your mouth shape.

Hot spot

"I find it difficult to encourage the children to talk about stories."

Children are often much more willing to become a character than adults. By answering questions as a character on the hot spot they can use their imagination or understanding of a story to explore feelings or situations.

Hot spotting can be used in a variety of situations with groups of varying sizes. You could try the ideas below following a group story or role-play activity.

- Identify a chair or carpet tile as the hot spot.
- Following a story, ask for a volunteer to sit on the hot spot to be a given character, for example the first pig in the 'Three Little Pigs'.
- You could give a prop or costume item to support the characterisation, for example straw for the first little pig.
- Start by asking very simple questions, for example 'what did you use to build your house?' For some children this may be enough. Praise their responses.
- Extend more able children by asking questions that relate to the feelings of the character. 'How did you feel when...?'
- Extend further by asking questions that take the character beyond the established story and into an imaginary situation. 'What would you do if...?'
- Once the pattern of question and answer is established, encourage other children to ask questions.

Teaching tip

Less confident children could take their turn on the hot spot in a pair or with an adult. Keep turns fairly short in order to maintain the interest of children in the group.

Taking it further

You could draw attention to the emotions felt by characters at different times by encouraging children to show facial expressions that reflect these feelings.

IDEA 38

Reflecting with photos

"We often take photos of the children and we print some off for our records but it would be nice if we could use them more with the children."

Photos can be used to engage children and help to develop their social and communications skills. They are also brilliant tools to aid reflection.

Teaching tip

Ensure that you have parental permission to use photographs of children.

Involving parents

Ask parents to send in photos of their child involved in activities at home. More able children may be able to talk about these to a group, others may prefer to talk to you individually. This helps the child to talk about things other than the here-and-now and may be an opportunity to introduce conversations about religious celebrations and differences between families.

Children love to look at photos of themselves and their friends. The following ideas suggest ways in which this natural interest can be used in an Early Years setting.

- Take time to look at recent photos with individual children. Ask them to select one or two and describe what was happening in the picture. Listen to their responses, allowing them sufficient time to think, and prompt with open questions.
- The children's comments could be recorded and could be used as part of your evidence gathering. You may well gain information on a child's learning characteristics and their abilities to reflect on their own learning.
- Photos of a child involved in a self-initiated activity provide a perfect opportunity to engage in simple conversation that is relevant and of interest to the individual. Trying to have a conversation with a child who is engrossed in an activity can interrupt their concentration. The photo will act as a reminder of a familiar and enjoyable activity and can help the less confident child to talk.
- Some children find it difficult to make the eye contact that often precedes an interaction. Using a photo to initiate a conversation releases the child from the need to make the initial eye contact and may reduce anxieties and promote speech.

48

I'll huff and I'll puff!

"One of the children started blowing bubbles in his milk with a straw. It made such a mess."

Controlling the speed, strength and duration of breath is an important skill for speech production. Forming the lips to blow in a particular direction or to seal around a straw or whistle can strengthen the muscles and practise lip shaping for the production of some sounds.

The aim of the following ideas is that they should be fun and therefore motivate children to persevere, developing the control necessary for clear, regulated speech. Many of the activities are visually interesting and provide a perfect opportunity for language development.

- Bubble painting is easy and effective. Pour a small amount of washing up liquid into a cup and then half fill with a mix of water and paint. Give a straw to a child and check that they are able to blow. Ensure that the child takes a deep breath (this reduces the chances of sucking rather than blowing!) before blowing. When bubbles rise above the lip of the cup, place a piece of paper onto the bubbles to make a print.
- Give children straws to blow small pieces of tissue paper or ping-pong balls around the floor. This can be made into a game by adding plates to land the paper on or goals for the balls.
- Blow winter tree pictures by placing a blob of runny paint onto some paper (sugar paper will be too absorbent for this), and chasing it across the sheet by blowing behind the droplet. It will leave twig-like shapes.
- Make simple pinwheels or tissue paper strands on sticks to explore the effect of blowing and then stopping.

Teaching tip

Children will often find it difficult to regulate their blowing and may become breathless or dizzy. Encourage children to take short turns with these activities.

Where?

"I asked him to put the cups next to the sink. It took me ages to find them!"

A secure understanding of positional language can help a school child to follow instructions without misunderstandings.

Children will often follow instructions to place an item in, on or under when the position is the expected one, for example put the puzzle pieces **in** the box, put the teddy **on** the chair, but they may be responding to their experience rather than an understanding of the specific language. Try some of the ideas below to practise and extend comprehension.

- Practise responding to under or in by providing a selection of bags, boxes, cups, or purses and asking children to find a small item by listening to instructions.
- Play short nonsense games by placing a few, unrelated items on the table. Model placing a teddy or toy on or under the items and clearly state the position. Ask each child in turn to follow an instruction. Extend the activity by introducing in, next to, behind and in front.
- Select books that involve positional language and draw attention to the related actions of the characters.
- Adapt 'Simon Says' to include positional language. Ask children to make suggestions for actions.

Drama games – listening

"The children love games that make them laugh, and if they learn to listen at the same time, that's even better."

Fun and games motivate children to engage and listen. Practising attention skills in isolation can become monotonous and so group games that children enjoy can be the perfect means to improve listening, understanding and attention.

Play these games with groups of different sizes and of mixed abilities. You could play several games in a session, keeping games short in order to maintain the interest of the children.

- Stand or sit in a circle. Model and then encourage children to throw or roll a ball to a child across the circle, establishing brief eye contact or exchanging a smile before releasing the ball. On receipt of the ball the child says 'I have the red ball'. This becomes a drama game when you take away the real ball and replace it with an imaginary ball. Children need to focus their attention on the child with the imaginary ball to follow its path.
- Individual or pairs of children move around a defined space without touching any other child. Use a tambourine or bell to indicate that children should stop and then say a word to describe the action required. You could choose facial expressions, an animal or a body shape (wide/tall/short).
- The Magic Wand game can again be adapted to suit the learning needs and levels of the children. First, introduce your magic wand (a pencil with tinsel on the end will be fine). Play some music and ask the children to move around to this. Stop the music and cast your spell, turning the children into different materials such as wood, jelly, bubbles etc., different animals, vehicles or whatever you choose.

Teaching tip

Encourage children to listen by whispering your spells or by telling them that you can only say it once.

Taking it further

See if you can mime instructions to your group, they'll love trying to guess what you're saying. Make your actions as exaggerated as you can and the children will find it hilarious.

Learning with books

Part 6

Books? Where?

"I never know where to put the books. They usually end up getting trodden on."

Children who spend time looking at and handling books at a young age are more likely to have developed some of the pre-reading skills necessary to learn to read by the time they start school.

Taking it further

A group trip to your local library will encourage children to look at books on display. Many libraries also have story sessions you could attend. Following a trip, you could make a role-play library in your setting.

Bonus idea ★

Unfortunately books that are well-used by young children rarely last long. Rather than offering tired, taped-up books, replenish your shelves by visiting charity shops or asking parents to donate a book at Christmas.

Ensure a provision of books is freely accessible to the children in your setting. If you feel that some children are not showing a great deal of interest in books, try some of the following ideas.

- Ensure that your setting has a variety of fiction and non-fiction books and that they are stored in child height locations.
- Most children's books have been carefully designed to make the front cover appealing. Make the most of this by displaying some books with the front cover showing. There are a variety of stands available to allow this, but if money or space is short, put books on a table or covered box.
- Change your display of books each day. You could select them with a common theme.
- Make a Brilliant Book Box. This could be as simple as a decorated cardboard box. Each day put in a book with appealing illustrations and monitor the interest that this generates.
- An out of reach shelf could be used to store special books that are delicate. Some pop-up books will not survive an Early Years environment for long but can be enjoyed with adult supervision. This can also help to develop an understanding that books should be handled with care and can be a treat.

Which book?

"He always chooses the same book, the one with the sound buttons."

It can be almost impossible to predict which books might interest young children and it can be surprising which ones will become firm favourites!

With the increasing use of electronic readers among adults, children see fewer people reading real books and there may be few in their homes. The ideas that follow aim to develop children's interest in books and provide a varied experience of early reading.

- Aim for a balance of fiction and non-fiction books.
- Consider the interests of the children when selecting new books, especially non-fiction. You may be able to encourage an interest in reading through a subject of trains or animals.
- Books created from television programmes can engage young children but often lack the simple storylines and subtle choice of language present in many picture books.
- Check that the range of books reflects a multicultural society.
- Some children can find it difficult to interpret detailed illustrations, while others will love to search for hidden images. Ensure that you provide a balance of photographic and hand-illustrated texts.
- Young children are often drawn to books with textures included in the illustrations or books with flaps to lift. Try to offer a variety of each to broaden these children's experiences.

Teaching tip

Sound books can be useful to engage a reluctant child, but can become annoying to adults and other children. The sound buttons can also distract from the illustrations and text. If a child likes these books, try moving them on to the shared reading of books that invite sound making, such as animal or emergency vehicle books.

Involving parents

You could introduce a day, maybe once a month, when children bring in a favourite book from home or their local library. Encourage parents to talk to their child about the book before they bring it in.

Big books

"Big books are good because all the children can see the pictures but I'm never sure how to use them to teach the children to read."

Big books can be a wonderful resource to use with groups of young children. Through modelling and questioning adults can teach basic book knowledge and through participation and interaction, children can practise their skills.

Taking it further

Many of the ideas here can be used with non-fiction books. Think about the children's interests and choose topics that will appeal to them.

The reading abilities within any group will vary greatly. Story sessions using big books can be differentiated to meet varied needs through targeted questioning and appropriate support.

• Be careful not to spoil the story by focussing on too many teaching points in one session. If children don't enjoy the session, they are unlikely to learn anything.
• Use language such as front cover and title incidentally while introducing the book.
• You could hold the book the wrong way up or round and wait for children to correct you.
• Ask children to anticipate the story content from the illustration on the front cover.
• Point to the text as you read the words, demonstrating that the words are read from left to right, top to bottom.
• Indicate the page to be read, indicating left page before right.
• Talk about illustrations.
• When reading stories with repetition, encourage children to join in.
• Encourage children to use illustrations to anticipate the end of sentences.
• Occasionally ask a child to indicate where to read next.
• Ask children to anticipate the ending of the story. If the children are familiar with the storyline then they can be encouraged to include some detail.
• Point out any speech bubbles or labels.

Bonus idea ★

Invite the children to tell their own story based on the illustrations in the big book. This will reinforce the idea that the pictures describe the story and also encourage them to pay attention to the smaller details on the pages.

Snuggle up and read

"If he's tired, all he wants to do is cuddle up next to me with a book."

It is lovely for adults and children to spend time together looking at books and it is a shame if this only happens when children are tired or seeking comfort.

Providing an inviting reading area can encourage children to take an interest in sharing books even when they are at their most lively. While some of the ideas below require an amount of space not available in all Early Years settings, they could be adapted. You may find that you can involve the children in designing and creating a reading area that will be unique.

- Make sure that there are comfortable places to sit near to your books. This will encourage children and adults to use the area. You may have a large squashy sofa, a few beanbags or a pile of cushions.
- If your selection of seating is limited, try placing a soft blanket over hard seats.
- We all spend time adapting role-play areas to suit topics, so why not try a similar makeover for your reading area. For example, a display of stories and non-fiction books about train travel placed next to a train with a line of carriages may invite the reluctant reader. Introducing the area as the Reading Train will highlight its intended use. Other ideas could include a castle, a rocket or a boat.
- When the weather is good, place mats and cushions in shaded areas outside, with books clearly displayed.
- The space under a table covered by a thin cloth can make a great, secret reading den. Just make sure that there is sufficient light to see the book!

Stories from pictures

"Some children seem to find it really difficult to think of their own ideas. They usually wait for someone else to suggest something and then copy them."

It is extremely difficult to teach a child to be a creative thinker, but we can support them by providing prompts and choices that will allow a child to influence the direction of a storyline.

Teaching tip

Some children may respond better to objects rather than photos or pictures. Put together a box of items for these children to select, handle and consider their part in the story instead. A lamp, coin or feather could alter the story and engage the child.

As a child becomes confident in making supported choices, they will begin to generalise their skills, in independent small world play, in group role-play and eventually in drama and creative writing. The following ideas can be adapted to suit a variety of themes and topics and, with differentiated support, are suitable for children of different abilities. Sessions should be short to begin with but, if children are keen, could be extended.

- Gather together photos or drawings of settings such as a wood, a castle, a beach, a variety of houses, a zoo and a farm. These can be found in magazines, books or downloaded from the Internet. If you are able to mount and laminate these you will be able to use them repeatedly.
- Collect pictures of characters and some familiar objects such as toys, food, furniture and treasure boxes.
- Keep sets of images in separate folders. You could mount each set on a different colour card to make sorting them at the end of the session easier.
- Work with a small group and begin by explaining that you are going to make a story together. It is important that children are told that everyone will have a turn and that listening to each other is part of the activity.

- Spread the setting images in front of the group and ask one child to choose a picture. Differentiate questioning and prompting to gain more information about the setting. This could include the weather, time of day, size of castle, the feeling of the wood.
- Ask the next child to select a character and build on this as before. If children struggle to add detail, model the activity using clear, familiar ideas. Children with language difficulties may need more images at this point to indicate their choices, such as happy/sad/grumpy faces.
- The events in the story can be led by finding objects or meeting other characters.
- Children may need support to bring the story to a satisfying close initially.
- The story could be recorded digitally, written by hand or left unrecorded.
- Finish the activity by retelling the whole story. Children may like to draw illustrations to accompany their work. You may even be able to tell your group story to other children or parents.
- Children will benefit from participating in this type of activity several times as their confidence to give ideas will increase and the modelling that they hear from others may inspire new thoughts.

Taking it further

Stories can be extended further by adding pictures of types of transport; consider using rockets, space ships, a school bus or a shopping trolley!

Bonus idea

Throw something unexpected into the mix and ask the children how they think the to relate to feelings and emotions, as well as encouraging them to consider even more creative ideas.

Books with props

"Some of my group just aren't interested in listening to stories. They look all around the room or just wander off."

When reading stories in large groups, some children will maintain attention, gaining an understanding and real enjoyment of the story, but others will struggle. In these situations, real objects can often be used very effectively.

Using puppets and toys to act out a story as you read it from a book is a wonderful way to engage children and to help them to understand a basic storyline. As a child's understanding of stories develops, it will rely less heavily on the props and more on the text and illustrations.

- Plan which book you will read in advance and prepare your resources. Children rarely question the proportions of your props, so don't worry if you are reading a book about a boy and a dog and you can only find a small plastic boy and a large cuddly dog!
- Decide which parts of the story are the most important or interesting and collect a few more resources for these parts. If the characters go for a picnic, try to find a piece of fabric and some play food.
- Sit on the floor or low to the ground as it will be easier to manage your props. If possible, sit your group in a horseshoe shape in front of you so that they can all see the book and the space in front of you.
- If you have a bookstand they can be useful to keep the book visible and your hands free.
- Keep your props behind you or in a box. They need to be easy to find without being a distraction.

- If the setting of the story is important, a few coloured fabrics can indicate a change of location. A piece of blue fabric spread flat works well for the sea, or scrunched into a line for a river, a flat sheet of green for a field or placed over a box for a hill. These can be set out before you begin. Be careful not to put the edges of fabric close to any child who is likely to fiddle with them!
- Introduce your main characters before you begin reading.
- There is no need to read and use props concurrently. This would distract from the book itself when we are aiming to enhance it. Read a page or section, pause and illustrate that part with the objects.
- Some children may be able to retell the story at the end using the objects.

Taking it further

You could make up story bags for traditional tales or favourite books. These are sold commercially but can be expensive. You may be able to persuade some creative parents to help you create some bags of props that will be readily available to use at story time.

Bonus idea

Glove puppets are great to use but can restrict you from turning pages etc. Having introduced the puppet on your hand, they can be placed over a water bottle or tin can to stand on the floor until you need them again.

Reading aloud

"The others all do funny voices and make the sounds when they read to the group, I just feel really embarrassed."

Reading a book to a group of children isn't as easy as just saying the words and showing the pictures. In order to engage and maintain their interest you need to bring the book to life.

We can't all be actors, confident with speaking in different accents and voices, but the ideas below may help you to find a way in which you can involve your young audience in a story without feeling uncomfortable.

- Pre-read the book before the group story session. Knowing what will happen will help you to ask appropriate questions and respond to children's ideas and answers.
- Ensure that all children can see and are comfortable before you begin.
- Set the scene of the story before you start. A simple 'this is a story about a mouse who lives on a farm. Have you been to a farm? What might we find on a farm?' will help to engage the children before you begin.
- Vary the volume and pace of your reading. A slow quiet voice before an exciting part of the story creates suspense and encourages the children to focus. Save your loudest voice for the surprise 'BANG' or 'NO'.
- If you don't like attempting other accents and voices, simply vary your pitch to suit a character.
- Change your facial expression to reflect the emotions of the characters in the story. If you don't feel comfortable with this, choose a confident child to do this for you. Most of the children will copy!

Preparing to write

Part 7

Looking at marks

"He holds a crayon and scribbles but he looks around the room when he's doing it."

Until a child's attention is focussed on the marks they are making, they will be unable to make progress in drawing and writing.

For many children, the busy nursery environment makes it difficult to maintain attention on the mark making activities that develop the early skills necessary for writing and representational drawing. The ideas below are possible in most Early Years settings and aim to engage a child's interest whatever their level of development in this area.

- Provide a variety of mark making resources each day. Observe the features (size, colour etc.) that attract individual children and use this knowledge to engage those children that you have identified as needing support.
- Be aware that some children will find it difficult to hold and maintain the firm grasp and consistent pressure necessary to succeed with pencils and crayons. Large felt pens, dry wipe boards and paint produce clear, satisfying marks with little pressure.
- Position mark making activities in a variety of situations, quiet areas, busy spaces, indoors and outside. Note where children choose to engage in these tasks.
- Encourage children to draw on large sheets of paper on the floor while on their hands and knees. This position directs their attention towards the paper and the marks that they produce.
- Work collaboratively, hand over hand, making large marks in paint or felt pens. Talk enthusiastically or make sounds like whoosh... wee... wow! to demonstrate your interest in the activity.

Copy cat writing

"There are always pencils and paper available, but the children hardly ever try to write."

Children love to copy adults and this is often how they learn new skills. Modelling the process of writing in various real and play situations is a good way to engage young children in writing as a means of recording.

Don't worry if your writing is not clear or perfectly formed for the activities below, the aim is to demonstrate that writing is used for a purpose and is created (in English) by making marks on the paper from left to right and top to bottom. Writing in other languages is equally valid.

- Model writing in role-play areas; take an order in a role-play café; write a shopping list, a phone message or a birthday card.
- When writing a narrative observation on a Post-It note, try to work at child level so that children can watch you write. If they show interest, briefly explain that you are writing to help you remember later the things that you see.
- Many Early Years settings have books through which parents and key workers communicate. If children show interest when you are writing in these, ask if the child would like to write about something they have done. Allow any mark making and annotate yourself so that parents can understand their child's message.
- Use language associated with writing whenever appropriate (words, list, letters, full stop etc.). While it is unlikely that children will fully understand these terms, familiarity with the words will support later learning.
- Write birthday cards to children and staff in front of the children.

65

Guess which hand!

"He will have a go at writing his name but he swaps the pencil from hand to hand."

Some children will develop a dominant hand before they make any attempt at writing, others will be undecided for many years. Children should not be forced to use one hand or the other during their Early Years and may use a different hand to hold a pencil than they use for scissors.

While young children should not be forced to commit to a preferred hand, they should be encouraged to use and strengthen their hands to develop their fine motor control. As fine motor skills develop, most children will naturally find that one hand is easier to use than the other.

- Make sure that scissors and tools are suitable for both left and right-handed use. Try cutting with scissors not suited to your own hand preference to experience the difficulties a child may face.
- When beginning a task, always place the pencil, scissors or tool centrally in front of the child. Observe which hand they use to pick up the item.
- Encourage children to undertake two-handed tasks such as threading beads or pasta.
- Introduce activities that require the pulling of a rope, cord or hosepipe. Children could be fire fighters pulling in their hose or sailors pulling a cardboard box boat across the sea. Teach children who do not naturally pull hand over hand to do this.

Taking it further

Observe children in a variety of situations. It is interesting to identify if a child has a dominant foot to kick a ball or climb steps although this may not always link to the eventual dominant hand.

Outdoor writing

"I know that we are supposed to encourage children to write outside as well as inside, but it's difficult. The paper just blows away."

As children develop their understanding of writing and its uses, it is possible to provide a variety of opportunities for incidental emergent writing outdoors as well as inside. Children will want to write and will develop a 'can do' attitude.

Providing opportunities to write outside requires a bit more imagination than indoors, but is nevertheless important; it broadens the experiences of the keen writer and can attract the more reluctant.

- In gardening areas, or role-play garden centres, provide pencils or pens and lolly sticks to write plant labels. You will need to model this initially.
- Provide clipboards and pencils for role-play builders.
- Write labels and signs for a garage.
- Small notebooks can be used for role-play police who control the bike traffic.
- Chalks, pencils and pens can be used to write on roof slates or pebbles. If you pre-write children's names as examples, they will be encouraged to look for their name and attempt to write on other pebbles.
- Work with the children to make traffic signs for bike and scooter areas.
- Write invitations for a teddy bears' picnic.
- Make lists of birds or wildlife that you see; this could be an ongoing record, kept over several weeks.
- Take photos of different areas of the outside environment and encourage children to use emergent writing beneath the pictures. These could be used for various games and treasure hunts.

Involving parents

Parents may need support in understanding that the squiggles produced by their children, in an attempt to write, are an important stage in writing development and deserve praise and encouragement.

Early Maths

Part 8

Talking Maths

"I want a not big one."

A basic understanding of mathematical language is a fantastic grounding for starting school. Key mathematical words are valuable not only as a secure base for mathematical learning, but also in everyday life such as playing games and asking for lunch!

Teaching tip

Remember that the basic concept of big and small must be established before the comparative and superlative language of bigger, biggest and smaller, smallest.

Children usually gain an understanding of basic mathematical language through day to day experience and carefully planned continuous play provision. It can also be useful to introduce sessions in which practitioners focus their observations on listening for and promoting this language.

- Stick up a list of key mathematical words on the wall of your setting, as a reminder for you to use them in your everyday provision.
- Introducing the concept of 'less' or 'fewer' can be tricky. Fruit and drink times can be a good opportunity to look at and compare volume, size and quantity.
- Differentiating between one and lots can be introduced with greatly contrasting numbers, providing clear visual clues. Encouraging children to link the word one with holding up a single finger helps them to generalise the concept. Offering a choice of one or lots of raisins can be a good motivator.
- Labelling shapes can be difficult as each label covers a wide variety of sizes. It is important to offer a variety of sizes when introducing shape so that children can begin to appreciate the range described by the label.
- Cooking is a good way to introduce the word 'add', and other language relating to volume.
- Growing cress or beans is a good way to work on the language of size.

Involving parents

Many parents are keen to help their child but are unaware that mathematical language can be practised so easily. Why not send home a mathematical word or concept of the week with suggestions as to how they could be introduced.

One by one

"He points to the objects but he counts much faster than he moves his finger."

Children often learn to count aloud by rote through learning number songs and rhymes. When learning to count, children need to break down the series of sounds into separate number words and link these individually to an item.

Providing a variety of experiences can help a child to develop their ability to say one number name for each item in a group. Activities can be adapted to link to topic areas and children's individual interests and can be introduced through adult participation in play as well as short, led activities.

- When counting aloud, leave a clear gap between number words.
- Make the numbers even more distinct from each other by clapping in between the number names.
- Link saying number names with large, whole body movements such as jumping from one hoop to the next or climbing steps.
- Count when stacking bricks. You may need to work hand over hand to initiate the movement-word timing.
- In a circle, support children to say one number name each as you pass an object around. Adjust the group size according to the abilities of the children and place less able children near the beginning of the count.
- Model a clear count with a clear movement when handing out cups or fruit at snack time.

Teaching tip

Use a child's chosen activity to count. A line of footballs can be kicked in time to a count, role-play food can be counted onto a plate or a handprint made each time a number is said.

Involving parents

Give some ideas for counting to parents and carers such as steps on the slide at the park; apples into bags at the supermarket; potatoes into a pan, and ask them to send in photos or write on a card the items counted. These could be displayed on a pin board and might encourage others to do the same.

How many?

"At fruit time, she counts and points at the cups in time but still can't tell me how many there are."

The majority of children who start school will be able to say how many items are in a small group. But for some children, the understanding that the final number said is the label for the number in that group is not always achieved without support.

It is easy to assume that a child who responds to the question 'how many?' by pointing to items one at a time and saying a number name for each, is able to count, but some children, who are then asked 'so how many are there?' will either begin to count again, or will give the next number in the sequence. Use these ideas to support a child to give an accurate final count.

- When modelling counting, emphasise the final number in the sequence and then state the number of items, for example, one, two, three, **four**. There are four ducks.
- Use body parts to establish one and two as a final count. For example, after singing 'Head, Shoulders, Knees and Toes' or 'Two Little Hands', say 'I have two ...?' for children to complete. Children are often motivated by looking in mirrors or watching others.
- Work with groups of one, two or three and state the number without counting first, using it as a label. Ask questions such as 'which boat has two bears in it?'
- Play finger games, showing a number of fingers, saying how many and counting afterwards.
- Occasionally start by saying how many items you have before counting them out.
- Demonstrate that the number of items in a group remains constant however the items are arranged.

Knowing numbers

"That's a number 'S' for Sophie."

It can be difficult for young children to differentiate between the different marks that they see around them. Letters and numbers, to the untrained eye, look very similar. It is often the context in which they are seen that gives the clue.

It is important, when supporting children to recognise numbers, to teach not test. It is tempting to point to a number and ask a child to identify it. If a child already knows the number then you are teaching them nothing, if they don't know it then they are bound to fail. Teaching doesn't need to be really formal; in its basic form it is a continued awareness of the environment with good adult modelling.

- Ensure that numbers displayed in the environment are clear. Many popular fonts have a closed four (4), which looks quite different from a handwritten four, and a curled nine that many children mistake for a six. While children will need to recognise these eventually, they can make initial learning difficult.
- While singing number songs, point along a number line or at number cards.
- Use the word numbers to describe the group of symbols in a variety of contexts such as role-play phones, tills, and calculators.
- Encourage children to look carefully at the shape of numbers by using matching activities, for example, bikes with numbers attached can be parked in numbered bays; numbered bean bags can be thrown into numbered boxes. Children do not need to be able to name individual numbers in order to match them up.

Taking it further

Take photos of numbers in different contexts, for example, on mobile phones, car number plates, doors, buses, cooker timers, clocks, and make them into an interactive display in your setting. Ask children to match the photo showing the numbers with the object on which they can be found.

Involving parents

Ask parents to help children to spot numbers on their journey. They may see house numbers, car number plates or numbers in shop windows.

Numbers for the more able

"I don't want to count the ducks again. I know there are five."

Differentiating activities to suit the needs of all children can be difficult but failure to do so can lead to poor behaviour and able children not being stretched enough. While some children like and need more repetition, some more able children may become bored and frustrated.

Simple changes to number skills activities can make them challenging and rewarding to the more able children in the group.

- When singing number rhymes, ask a more able child to use a whiteboard to keep a tally of the number of ducks, cakes or frogs.
- When reading number stories, ask some children to select matching number symbols as the book progresses, creating a number line as they do so.
- When pegging items on lines, challenge a child to predict how many items there may be before checking by counting. They may initially find this difficult, especially accepting that an incorrect guess can still be a good guess. It is a good idea to join in, making mistakes as you go.
- When working with sequences of numbers, cover one up and ask them to guess which is hidden.
- When playing simple step-taking games along a numbered track, ask children which number will come next or has just been passed.
- When threading beads or counting apples into a bag in a role-play shop, ask children how many there would be if one more were added or one taken away.

How big?

"It's a very tall snake."

Understanding size and the language associated with it is far from straightforward. An object is generally only big or small, long or short, wide or narrow when compared to another similar object. Some children may recognise that a teddy is big, because their experience tells them that most teddies are smaller than the one they see. Other children may only recognise it as big when a smaller one is placed directly beside it.

Try to provide opportunities for comparing size and work on early skills involved in measuring. All these activities can be fun and introduced through play-based learning.

- Provide different sized clothes and a variety of dolls. Talk to children about which clothes would be suitable for which doll and the reasons for this.
- Read stories about size; maybe also follow on from these with artwork. Try to make sizes contrasting, for example elephants and mice or trees and flowers.
- Provide a variety of different sized boxes and items to put inside. This could be introduced through a role-play shop or wrapping presents for a teddy's birthday.
- When playing outside, measure a road for the bikes or running track by counting strides.
- Make lists of things that are bigger or smaller than the children.
- When offering fruit, ask the child to select a size of portion.
- Collect natural objects and compare their sizes and shapes.

Taking it further

For more able children, introduce non-standard measure using hand-spans, footprints or bricks.

Bonus idea ★

Make flowers that are the same height as individual children, and adults! They make a lovely display and provide a perfect opportunity to explore size.

Money, money, money

"I hardly ever have cash, I always pay with my card."

While cards as payment and internet shopping should not be ignored in early education, children need to develop an understanding that items can be bought using coins and notes.

The ideas below will help children to develop their understanding of the use of money to buy and sell, and to recognise that coins are not all the same.

- Encourage children to play role-play shop. Vary the type of shop to engage the interest of more children. You could try selling food, toys, clothes, shoes, hats and bags, books, or an optician or post office.
- Allow children to look into your purse or wallet, giving money some real context.
- If possible, arrange for children to buy items during a trip out. Take photos of the till and shop to use when talking about role-play shops in your setting.
- During song time, sing 'One Current Bun' and allow children to buy a bun using a real coin. This will introduce a simple exchange of a coin for an item. Ask children to suggest other things that could be bought and adapt the song to match.
- Coins can be stuck to a table surface using double-sided tape. If you stretch paper over the table you can make rubbings using crayons. Foil stretched over the table can be rubbed to discover the coins below. Children will begin to notice similarities and differences between coin types.

Time for time

"My tooth falled out next Wednesday."

Children need to understand that some things are happening now, some things have already happened and some things are yet to begin.

Very few children in Early Years settings will be ready to learn to tell the time, but they will all need to continue to develop their concept of time and the language associated with it in the short and long term. Much of this understanding depends on language and familiarity with routines and can be supported by gentle reinforcement to help the understanding to be generalised and secure.

- Try to be clear in your use of now and soon. Children will be confused if they are told that something will happen now or soon but it doesn't in fact happen for some time.
- There are a number of songs that include the days of the week. One could be sung each morning before identifying the day. 'Yesterday it was... so today it is...'. Challenge more able children by asking which day it will be tomorrow and including months and dates in a similar way.
- When growing plants, take photos at different stages of growth. Use these pictures to demonstrate use of time-related language (next, after that, later, before).
- Make displays of photos of children and staff showing different ages. Include labels and talk about a long time ago and now.
- When talking about plans for the day, refer to a visual timetable if possible, and use words like now, next, then and after that.
- Talk about seasonal changes as you see them and link them to the names of the seasons.

Teaching tip

When learning to tell the time, children usually start to tell the 'o'clock' times first. If possible, time events such as fruit time and story time to coincide with 11, 12, 1 o'clock etc, drawing attention to the time and how it is represented on a clock.

Taking it further

While children may not be ready to tell the time formally, play clocks can be included into role-play areas and imaginary times included in play. For example, 'the puppet show starts at 10 o'clock'.

Fun with shapes

"If I push this one it goes and goes. This one doesn't work."

Through play involving shapes, children will learn to recognise similarities and differences between groups of two and three-dimensional forms, and will hopefully develop an interest in exploring their qualities independently, using their knowledge when tesellating, constructing or collaging.

Once a child is familiar with handling and exploring shapes, learning to name and sort them is easier to achieve.

- Try having boxes of two-dimensional shapes available for children to access. Children may use them to represent food or money in a role-play or may spontaneously lay them out on a table or floor. Encourage, where possible, by joining in with their play.
- Cut a shape into the flat surface of a potato half for free printing.
- Provide solid three-dimensional shapes for printing. Children will begin to see the shapes of each of the faces.
- When cooking, use cutters to create circular, triangular or square biscuits, sandwiches or pizzas. When offering children this food, ask them to select their preferred shape.
- Some children may enjoy a shape hunt, looking for a given shape in the environment. Children could take photos of their findings.
- Provide a variety of three-dimensional shapes (boxes, balls and tin cans are fine) and a slope. Encourage children to find out which will roll and which won't.
- Build towers, exploring how a cylinder can be included but a sphere presents problems.

Bonus idea ★

You could introduce a shape table that focuses on one shape a week. Encourage children to place appropriate items or photos of larger objects on the table. Try to include tangible items for the children to touch, and examples of the shapes in the real world.

Odd one out

"She said it was the banana that didn't go because it's yellow. I said it's the broccoli because I don't like it!"

Identification of the odd one out can be introduced as a game, an adult-led group session or as part of tidy up time.

Recognising that an item doesn't belong in a group of similar items (and the reason why) can be explored on many levels. At its most simple, children can learn to group items together by matching or using a common theme, and isolate one that does not have the same characteristics. These skills will be useful in areas of Maths, science and arts and can support the development of language, particularly precision and description.

- Initially, make sure that the item to be identified is clearly different, for example a small teddy mixed in a bag of balls.
- Once the idea of spotting the odd one out is established, introduce some similarities to the odd item, for example a round, red counter amongst coins.
- As soon as a child appears confident with a selection, ask them to say why the item doesn't fit with the group. If they find this difficult, model an answer.
- As similarities between items increase, there could be more than one correct answer depending on the possible links identified between the items. It could be obvious to you that the green button does not fit in a group of blue buttons, but a child may select the only one with four holes. Give time for a child to justify their selection. They may have spotted a link that you have missed!
- Introduce activities that involve sorting by texture, smell, sound or taste to encourage children to explore items using all their senses.

Making Maths games

"The Maths games in the shops are so expensive and they never seem to be quite what you want."

Children usually find games motivating and will often be happy to repeat and practise simple tasks over and over, reinforcing their understanding and gradually extending their skills in order to complete the game.

Teaching tip

Some children may be motivated to play Maths games when they involve the use of familiar characters. Cut them from comics or books that have become torn or tatty and use them as counters or on boards. Another good idea is to mount the characters onto headbands or badges and ask children to 'become' them.

Homemade Maths games are not only cheaper but can also be adapted to meet the changing learning needs of the children in your cohort. The ideas below describe possible games that do not require too much time to prepare and most can easily be differentiated for more or less able children.

- Prepare some basic resources that can be used in a variety of Maths games. These could include three or four sets of laminated number cards up to 10, 20, 100 depending on your cohort, large blank dice (these can be purchased fairly cheaply) and several long strips, marked into between 10 and 20 squares; these could be laminated paper, heavy fabric, strips of wood or plastic.
- Simple games that practise number recognition and counting can be created easily using the strips and dice. Select a topic of interest to the children and use counters that relate to this. Possible examples are plastic spiders for 'Incy Wincy Spider', small trains, small teddies, or dinosaurs. Adapt the dice by writing on clear number symbols, (young children may begin with one and two, while older children may work up to six). Sit children on the floor or around a table with their strips pointing towards the centre and place something in the middle that relates to the topic, for example, a paper cloud, station, picnic or food item. Take turns to roll the dice to race to the centre.

- The above game can be extended by adding two strips together, racing up and down the ladder or using two dice with dots to be counted together.
- Large-scale games, in which the children act as the counter along a track created out of hoops in a line, can interest a different group of children. Children can count the correct number of jumps as they progress towards the finish; again, this can be varied according to interests and topic.
- Place numbers in the hoops to introduce early adding skills. 'You are on number four and you will move on two. Which number will you land on?'
- Shapes in a feely bag can be used to decide the number of steps to move forward. Children will learn about the qualities of shapes as they count the sides to see how many places to move.
- Group games in which numbers or shapes are clearly displayed in different areas of an inside or outside space can encourage the fast recognition of shapes and number symbols. Simply draw a number or shape from the bag to call and children run to that area. A variation on this is that children choose to stand by an area, one is identified and the group in this area are either out or win a point.

Bonus idea

Coins placed along a track could be collected as the counter lands on a square. The winner could be the child with the highest value of coins at the end.

Full up

"I want it to be more full."

Most children will explore volume and capacity spontaneously as they pour water from pot to pot or fill a bucket with sand.

The practical exploration of capacity provides opportunities for learning in many areas. The dexterity required to pour water from one container to another develops fine motor skills and concentration. Problem solving skills are developed as children challenge themselves to tessellate shapes to fit into a space.

- When planning cooking activities, seek out recipes that can be measured in cups. Many American cookbooks use this as standard. Children can work together to decide whether a cup is full, and can hear, and use language relating to volume and capacity. Many play dough recipes are measured in cups.
- Provide clear containers in the water tray that vary greatly in their capacity. Coloured water makes it easier to see water levels within these. Challenge more able children to predict how many times you will need to pour all the water from a small bottle into a larger one to fill it.
- Work on a larger scale with children and hoops or large teddies in boxes. Children will love the challenge of trying to fit one more child into an already crowded hoop!
- In role-play shops provide different size bags. Ask children to select a suitable bag for their purchases. It is best if all bags can be of a similar appearance otherwise children tend to select the prettiest rather than the most suitable bag.

Bonus idea ★

It can be fun to offer a range of boxes with lids that vary in size and ask children to try to find a particular, familiar item hidden in one. Encourage the children to consider the size of the item and judge whether it would fit into a box before looking.

Get creative

Part 9

Natural art

"We often paint outside but it would be nice to use natural things in artwork."

When exploring the outside environment with children we often focus on their early scientific knowledge but self-chosen natural resources provide endless opportunities to explore shape, texture, pattern and form from a more artistic perspective.

The following ideas may well be messy but the enjoyment factor, together with the varied learning opportunities, should make the washing up and wiping down worthwhile!

- Make mud faces on tree trunks. Children will enjoy mixing the mud to make a malleable consistency. Pick up handfuls of mud and push it onto a tree trunk. Children can use fingers to mark the eyes and nose or they could find twigs, stones and leaves to make faces. Mud faces won't last for long so take photos for a record.
- Make hoop patterns. Give each child a hoop to place on the floor. Encourage them to collect natural items and arrange them in the hoop.
- Collect sticks and challenge children to make the tallest tower that they can.
- Make mini gardens in plastic food trays. Moss makes good grass, a twig can become a tree and stones can form a path. Children may like to add small toy figures or animals.
- Collect blackberries and use them to make a natural dye. Simply crush them with some white fabric and look at the colour changes. The colour won't be fixed without boiling.
- Make flowers using stones and leaves.

Teaching tip

Always remind children to wash their hands after handling natural objects.

Bonus idea

Make necklaces or headbands by threading petals and leaves onto threads. Encourage children to find as many different colours in the natural world as they can.

X marks the spot!

"The children love doing actions to songs. I'd like to take this further."

Drama and adult-led role-play can be used to explore a variety of curriculum areas and can help children to develop their skills in cooperation, listening and creativity.

Children often love creative drama sessions. While initially many children will rely on an adult to direct the action, children will soon feel confident enough to offer their own thoughts and suggestions. The following ideas can be used with children of mixed ability.

- Children love to go on a bear hunt! Hide a large teddy and move around the available space, acting out the way in which you would move through mud, grass, trees or other habitats. When you discover the bear, run back through all the areas and end by lying down, hiding under blankets.
- Adventures and treasure hunts allow children to make choices about a location and obstacles to negotiate along the way.
- Try creating a large journey map before you set off on your adventure. Draw a long, twisting line to represent the route and identify the destination at the end with a large X. Geographical features that will be encountered on the journey can be stuck along the route indicating the order in which the story will develop. Children can all take a turn to suggest an obstacle to stick on. This preparatory work will allow all children to be involved in the creative process, will avoid later arguments as to what will happen next and will give a visual picture of the story, helping to give an early understanding of beginning, middle and end.

Let's get messy!

"We were going to do footprints yesterday but I couldn't face the clearing up."

It is tempting to try to keep children clean to avoid hours of washing, wiping and clearing up, but carefully planned messy play can be enormous fun and can provide experiences that stimulate language, observation and physical skills.

The ideas below will require adult supervision but will also provide opportunities for spontaneous investigation and exploration. Involving children in the clearing up process develops their self-help skills and their ability to work together as well as reducing the clearing up after a session.

- Investigate colour mixing by dipping one hand in one of the primary colours and the other in a different one. When children rub their hands together they will produce a third colour. You could also try one coloured hand and one white hand to explore shades.
- Explore mark making on a smooth surface by drawing with fingers in shaving foam. Ensure that the surface is a different colour from the foam. Paint can be added to the foam if desired.
- Work outside to allow free exploration of materials. Children will love to mix materials. Try using flour, water, powder paint, glitter, rice, the options are endless. Try to observe and support rather than direct the exploratory play. You will probably need to limit the number of children taking part in this activity but you will attract many interested observers.
- Play with bubbles! Encourage children to use whisks and hands to create bubbles in the water tray. You can add washing up liquid or bubble bath to create fantastic foam that can be blown or shaken from hands.

Teaching tip

When children have messy hands, teach them to walk to the sink with their hands in the air so that they don't cover all their friends and furniture in paint, glue or foam as they go! Also, always check that children don't have any allergies to the perfumes or colourings in the items that you use.

Making marks outside

"I don't think I've ever seen him painting or drawing. He always wants to run around outside."

It is lovely to see children running, climbing and exploring the natural world and these activities can be encouraged and extended to support a developing interest in mark making.

Wind and rain make working on paper frustrating outside, and children will soon lose interest. Try some of these ideas to promote an interest in making lines, shapes and patterns, which will help to develop the motor skills and hand-eye coordination necessary for representational drawing and letter formation.

- Use chalks to draw on paving slabs, pebbles, roofing slates or shed walls.
- On dry days, paint with water onto walls. Vary the size of brushes on offer.
- When the ground is mostly dry encourage children to cycle or walk through puddles of water and look at the prints they leave. Brooms can be used to vary the marks left.
- Paint onto old sheets either on the ground or hung over a board. If it rains, encourage children to notice the effect and explore the possibilities. If there is no rain, you could spray, drip or pour water on the fabric.
- Draw with pencils, crayons or pens onto pieces of wood.
- Put sticks and combs into shallow sand trays. (Make sure that the tray base is a clearly different colour to the sand so that marks are visible.)
- If you have sufficient space, sprinkle flour trails onto grass to make patterns. You can mix powder paint into the flour for different colours. At the end of the session the flour can be washed away. Children will love to follow the trails.

Colouring in

"I know that people say we shouldn't give them pictures to colour in, but they do love it!"

Many people believe that giving children pre-drawn pictures can inhibit the development of independent drawing and limits creativity. However, it cannot be denied that many children love pictures of familiar items.

Familiar images can be used to engage and motivate a child in an activity in which they would usually show little interest. A variety of skills that are important in school are practised in the ideas listed below.

- Fine motor skills and pencil control, necessary for handwriting, can be developed by careful colouring within clear lines.
- Cutting around simple pictures develops scissor skills and finger strength.
- Careful selection of images, linked to interests such as transport or animals, may encourage children who are reluctant to engage in mark making activities to attempt to hold and control pens and pencils.
- If children are reluctant to draw independently, try giving a small pre-drawn image and encourage them to add additional features, for example add carriages on a train or fish to an underwater scene.
- Colouring long thin shapes such as snakes helps children to develop the skills involved in copying pre-writing patterns.
- Directional mark making can be practised by drawing over dotted outlines of shapes.
- Listening skills can be developed by giving verbal direction for colouring, for example colour the gloves blue and the hat red.
- Spatial awareness and motor planning can be supported through joining small items on a page with a pencil line.

Taking it further

Link colouring sheets to a topic and they can be used to form simple books. Ask children to think of captions to add to each picture to develop literacy skills.

Cross-curricular printmaking

"I sometimes include some printing in my creative planning. The children enjoy it."

Printmaking can be used to explore a variety of curriculum areas and can help children to engage in learning. Printmaking will appeal to the visual as well as the kinaesthetic learner.

The following ideas aim to demonstrate the diversity of topics that can be introduced, explored or practised through printmaking in the Early Years. Many can be adapted to link to other areas of learning.

- An interest in the natural world can be nurtured by making press prints with leaves. This will draw attention to the wide variety of shapes and sizes and draws attention to the vein formation on the back of a leaf.
- Mathematical patterns, especially those with regular repeats, can be explored through block prints with potatoes or sponges. This idea of a number of shapes in a repeat sequence can also be used to practise cooperation and turn-taking skills if each child in a group holds one block and they create a pattern together.
- Counting and set building can be practised by printing a requested number of images in an area, maybe three apples and seven bananas in a bowl. The action of making the mark will give a physical reinforcement of the one to one nature of counting.
- Differences in textures can be explored by painting an uneven surface then laying a piece of paper over it and rubbing the reverse of the paper with the back of a spoon. Descriptive language can be introduced and practised and comparisons between textures drawn.

Taking it further

Create your own topic-related blocks by cutting shapes out of card. Stick these shapes onto card tiles and then print from them by rolling paint onto the block and pressing onto paper. You will gain a clearer print if you apply pressure or rub with the back of a spoon or a large pebble.

Building pictures

"I say 'That was quick. Would you like to do another picture, Sam?' But Sam just walks away."

When children are working at the pre-representational stage of painting and drawing, it can be difficult to engage their interest in the task beyond a quick squiggle.

These ideas aim to provide a breadth of experiences that allow children to make creative choices when building pictures. They could be used to support story telling activities or topic work.

- Provide a choice of simple, pre-cut images that could be used to add to paintings and drawings. These could include animals, people, plants or buildings.
- Vary the shape and colour of paper on offer for free painting, drawing and collage. Black paper can be used with chalks or pigments mixed with white paint.
- Provide pages from magazines and newspapers for children to select images to add to their work.
- Occasionally, try offering paper with small images pre-drawn or stuck to it as part of your continuous provision. Observe the children's response to these and talk about their work with them. The images may help some children to recognise that marks can be used to represent items as they make their own additions to the picture.

Taking it further

Several of the ideas could be introduced simultaneously to increase the choices available for children, allowing greater individuality.

Start with a tube

"They just stick the boxes together. Lots of them can't tell me what they have made."

Children who have begun to think creatively before starting school will be able to approach many learning activities with confidence and imagination. Model making is a perfect opportunity to encourage early creativity.

The ideas that follow place an emphasis on the child's involvement in the creative process rather than a perfect end product. No two models will be identical and many will need a carefully planned display or a label to make the child's intentions clear.

- Try working with a small group. Present each child with a cardboard tube or box and allow time for this to be explored. Model the exploration by turning your tube in different ways, rolling it and looking through it. Listen for any comments or ideas that the children make spontaneously. Through open questions such as 'what could it be?' or picking up on gesture, establish what children would like to create.
- Introduce other boxes, card and paper and discuss the qualities of a few.
- Stay with children as they work to create their item. Remind children of their aim and talk about their choices of material, linking it to the intended item.
- Unstructured building may not always be appropriate but children can be given choices when following a more prescribed pattern. For example, when building rockets, children can shape a tight or open cone; they can make choices about colour, decoration and the size of fins.

Building dens

"I often find him under the display table. He makes a pile of cushions in front and peeps out."

Many children love to make and play in dens. The physical nature of the activity often attracts a different group of children than a traditional role-play area but can provide similar opportunities for creativity and collaboration.

These ideas aim to provide children with opportunities to create their own spaces without the need for large, expensive equipment.

- Large cardboard boxes are always a good start for creating spaces to hide and play. Try cutting child sized holes in the sides and sealing the tops. If you have several boxes with holes cut at similar heights, children will be able to crawl from one box into another.
- Rather than cutting holes, try cutting flaps that need to be lifted before crawling through.
- Children could paint the outside of their cardboard box den. Talk to the children to establish how they see their creation before helping them to make choices. If they hope to hide in their box then you could talk about camouflage. If they plan to have a party then bright colours may be more suitable.
- Large sheets of fabric can be thrown over tables or basic frames; duvet covers or curtains work really well. If possible, provide a selection of colours, textures and weights so that children can explore the different effects of the light that passes through the fabric.
- Sheets of cardboard make great walls for a 'table house', and can be easily taped to open and close as a door.

Taking it further

For some children the building of the den will be the motivation and they will lose interest before playing in it. Try to extend their creativity by joining them in games. If you don't fit inside, children will often be happy for you to look through their door!

Moving to music

"As soon as he hears the music he starts to jiggle around."

Children will often join an adult to march around the room to 'The Grand Old Duke of York' or join in with the actions to 'If You're Happy and You Know It'. These activities are fantastic for developing listening and physical skills and encouraging participation.

Consider the best ways for children with limited mobility to participate before the activity begins. Have ready any ribbons or scarves that may make small movements more prominent and ensure that the floor area is large enough for wheelchairs.

It can be interesting to video the responses of children to watch later. This can be useful when making detailed observations and children will love to see themselves dance. The comments that they make can also give an insight into their creative understanding.

Introduce some of these musical ideas into your setting.

- Collect a variety of music of different styles. You may include pop, jazz, classical, rock and music from different countries. Try to select a variety of fast and slow, loud and soft pieces.
- Try playing music as children paint. Play contrasting pieces and ask the children to paint a picture of the music.
- Play music outside as well as inside. Try playing music with a strong beat next to an area with brooms or balls that could be used to add to the rhythm.
- Gentle music can have a calming effect in areas that seem to attract boisterous behaviour.
- Play short samples of music when reading stories. For example, when reading a story based in Africa, play African music, or when reading about animals, play the relevant track from the Carnival of the Animals.
- Provide ribbons, pompoms and light scarves with music. Encourage children to move freely and use the resources.

Drama games

"Some children find it so difficult to think of their own ideas."

Simple group drama games can help children to develop their own ideas and imagination. Children can watch adults and more confident children and use these models to experiment with their own ideas in a safe, supportive environment.

- Simple, familiar games such as 'Duck, Duck, Goose' can be adapted to encourage imagination. Allow children to select which animal they would like to be and encourage them to fly, crawl or swim around the circle in the style of that animal.
- Miming games help children to develop their creativity through movement and also develop skills in speaking and listening as children ask and answer questions. Asking children to mime an action such as digging, brushing teeth or having a wash can be accompanied by questions such as 'when would you do this?' 'Do you do this every day?'
- 'The Car Journey' can be played with up to four children. Place two seats behind two others to create your car and give the driver a tin lid or other steering wheel. Ask the driver 'where are we going?' Then ask questions and encourage conversation with all children in the car about what you will take, what you will do when you arrive or what you might see. When conversation slows, call 'we're here!' Everyone gets out of the car and gets back in, sitting in a different position. The new driver selects the next destination.

Teaching tip

Some children may be unsure about taking an active role in the following games initially, but with time and appropriate support, children of all abilities can participate. More able children can develop their imaginations by offering their own suggestions and extending their ideas and actions.

Taking it further

You could work on short mimes, acting out a simple action such as buying an item from a shop or playing in a swimming pool. Encourage children to use their own ideas rather than rely on yours. Ask children to show their mime to their peers or parents.

Talking pictures

"I showed the children a painting of children playing. It was surprising how long they spent looking at it."

By providing a variety of opportunities for children to look, think and speak, we increase their ability to reflect on the things that they see and experience. Using examples of artwork is one way to develop observation skills while introducing children to the work of other artists.

While the suggested images can be viewed on a whiteboard it can be useful to print and laminate copies for children to handle and return to when they choose. The suggested paintings introduce a variety of styles and periods of artwork in order to provoke a variety of responses. You may like to look and talk about pictures with small groups or pairs of children in a quiet area of your setting.

Animals:
- Gwen John (1876-1939) Cats.
- George Braque (1882-1963) Birds.
- Henri Matisse (1869-1954) Birds (often in silhouette).
- Henri Rousseau (1844-1910) 'Tiger in a Tropical Storm' and 'Jungle with Lion'.
- George Stubbs (1724-1806) Horses and dogs.
- Albrecht Durer (1471-1528) Rhino and hare.
- Paul Klee (1879-1940) 'The Golden Fish', 'Around the Fish' and 'Fish Magic'.
- Rembrandt (1606-1669) Elephant drawings.
- Albert Cuyp (1620-1691) Cows and chickens.
- African Batik work – Various birds and animals native to Africa.
- Aboriginal art – Many fish, kangaroos and lizards.
- Various cave paintings.

Human activity:

- Pieter Bruegel (the Elder) (1525-1569) Children playing and adults working in different seasons.
- L.S. Lowry (1887-1976) People at work and in the streets.
- John Constable (1776-1837) 'The Hay Wain'.
- The Bayeux Tapestry.

Shape, colour and pattern:

- Wassily Kandinsky (1866-1896). Many examples contain concentric circles or triangles and lines that suggest movement. Colours are often bright and contrasting. These works can be good starting points for children's own work.
- Paul Klee (1879-1940) Regular and irregular shapes.
- Henri Matisse (1869-1954) Pattern in paintings and paper cuts.

Story starters:

- Richard Dadd (1817-1886) Fairies.
- Arthur Rackham (1867-1939) Fairies.
- Cicely Mary Barker (1895-1973) Flower fairies.
- Henri Rousseau (1844-1910) Habitats.
- John Everett Millais (1829-1896) 'Bubbles'.
- Katsushika Hokusai – 'The Wave' (Japanese wood cut).

Taking it further

Ask the children what they like and don't like about the pictures, whether they think the pictures are old or new, and whether the pictures make them feel happy or sad, or other feelings. The more able children might be able to identify reasons why the paintings make them feel certain things.

Bonus idea

If the children are interested in the artwork, they might like to try to draw their own versions. Consider creating a gallery for parents and carers to visit displaying the children's work alongside the artwork that gave them their inspiration.

Computer problems

"There are always problems around the computer. Some children hang around there the whole time and others never get a turn."

Some children are attracted to computers and will choose to play on one at any opportunity. Others show little interest, needing to be encouraged to take a turn. It can be difficult to establish a balance in an Early Years setting.

The following ideas may help to engage the children who show little interest in technology and suggest ways to limit the time spent on computers for some others.

- Different programs will interest different children. Paint programs, simple games or interactive stories can all teach skills in computer work.
- Many ICT skills can be learnt from battery operated toys and equipment. Children can learn to use switches or buttons to turn items on, off or draw links between the cause and effect of an action.
- Remote control toys can develop the precise use of controls. Challenges can be set up to extend the more able. Children will enjoy trying to knock cardboard tubes over using a remote control car.
- Sand timers placed next to a computer area can indicate when a child's turn should end.
- A list of names next to the computers, stuck to the wall using Velcro perhaps, could be used to indicate who has had their turn. These could be removed and posted into a box or stuck onto a separate list.

Taking it further

Children's digital cameras can now be purchased fairly cheaply and can be used in a wide variety of situations. This could be used to increase interest in the computer when images are viewed.

Inventing games

"The children love to play games, the sillier the better!"

When involved in a game, children will often persevere with challenging tasks in order to complete the course. Games are a fantastic means of encouraging children to practise social and turn-taking skills.

Adapt these ideas to suit the learning needs and interests of your cohort. Group sizes could be altered to provide support for those who need it and game lengths varied according to the levels of concentration of the children involved.

- Physical skills can be practised by drawing symbols on the sides of a blank dice or on cards representing an action, such as standing on one leg or jumping. Children can roll the dice or select a card and attempt the action. Another idea is that the cards could be placed along a track and the children perform an action when their counter lands there.
- Picture building games can be created for any topic. Portions of a picture are collected after rolling a dice or picking from a lucky dip, and an image is gradually built up.
- Large-scale games in which children move along a line of hoops can be adapted to relate to books and stories by adding objects to some of the hoops to indicate a reward or forfeit, e.g. in a 'Jack and the Beanstalk' game, some beans could indicate two extra steps forward, while a picture of a giant, or even a large welly, could demand a step back. For 'Three Little Pigs' include straw, sticks and a brick that could allow one, two or three steps forward and a wolf picture that demands that you return to the start.

Teaching tip

Encourage children to suggest ideas for games and rules. Among other skills, children will practise their speaking and listening skills and develop their creativity.

Cooking to learn

"They love to cook. I'd like to do more but I'm never sure how to justify it in my planning."

Many children, even those who show little interest in tabletop activities, will love to cook and will be happy to sit with a group until the task is complete. A wide variety of curriculum areas can be explored through cooking and, by varying the item to be made, children will be happy to repeat, practise and extend their skills.

Some of the possible curriculum links are shown below. These can be used when planning an activity to suit the learning needs of your cohort and can help when considering how to differentiate a cooking task to a group of children of mixed age or ability.

- Personal, Social and Emotional Development: Waiting, turn-taking and sharing equipment are all vital skills that can be modelled and practised.
- Communication and Language: Questions, responses and descriptive language are easily practised during a cooking activity. Specific language could include stir, rub in, separate, and these can be demonstrated to give meaning. Children will often be motivated by the activity to listen well and to respond to instructions.
- Physical Development: Many fine motor skills can be practised through cooking. Finger strength and dexterity, which are necessary for writing, will be developed when rubbing fat and flour together or picking up small items such as currants. Stirring will help to develop coordination and strength from the shoulder and breaking eggs and cutting requires a child to use both hands simultaneously.

- Literacy: Working from a recipe book or card will demonstrate that words carry meaning. Language such as list and instructions can be used when looking at the recipe and the type of book can be discussed.
- Maths: Counting the correct number of eggs or spoonfuls of flour will give a real context for counting. Comparing quantities using related language such as lots or full will again give a purpose for learning. Time and weight can be introduced at whatever level the children are working.
- Expressive Arts and Design: Allowing time to plan and discuss the position of items on a pizza, the decoration on a cake or the way in which to cut a sandwich will help children to learn to make creative decisions and judgements. Children can design their own fruit salads or smoothies and will often take great pride in the results.
- Understanding of the World: Drawing attention to the many changes in appearance can help children to develop skills of observation and description, for example, when mixing two items or before and after heating. Foods from different origins can promote discussion. Foods that link to festivals from different religions can encourage an interest in the lives of different people.

Involving parents

Encourage parents to cook with their children. You could ask them to bring in favourite recipes and develop your own cookery book. Copies could even be sold to raise money!

Bonus idea

Using chocolate in cooking sessions can be fun as well as a learning opportunity. Use its versatility to show children how it can be solid in a bar, melted to be a liquid, grated into a fine powder, and after melting it can set to be solid again. Remember to bear in mind any allergies when cooking and use sweet and sugary ingredients in moderation.

Learning through music

"Some children seem to be so motivated by music."

When working with children in the Early Years, it is important to follow their interests. Many children respond to music and this enthusiasm can be used to introduce a variety of skills that will form the foundations for future learning.

These ideas are quick to prepare and can be used individually or as part of a music session. They will be most effective with small groups.

- Develop counting skills by using a drum, triangle or any instrument with a short, clear sound. Sing or say 'listen for a number, listen for a number' and then play the instrument several times before asking children how many they heard. Vary the number according to the abilities of the children and alter the rhythm as children become more confident.
- Encourage children to think about materials and their qualities by providing a variety of instruments that are clearly wooden, metal or plastic, perhaps introducing two materials at a time. Listen to the sounds made by each of the individual instruments in the sets. Ask a child to select a material, and then all play an instrument from that group. Can children think of words to describe the sounds?
- Physical skills can be practised by making body percussion sounds. Ask children to make sounds such as clicking, clapping, slapping and tapping with their hands. Encourage them to explore the noises that they can make using their feet, legs or arms.
- Sound blending and segmenting can be practised through playing tuned or percussion instruments in time to word syllables. Children may like to start with names and then move on to animals, vehicles or instrument names.

Taking it further

Build a collection of multicultural instruments and use these to talk about other parts of the world. Think about music from around the world and play examples like Bluegrass country music from the USA or a Mariachi band from Mexico.

Exploring the world

Part 10

Bubbles with benefits

"They love playing with bubbles but I'm not sure what they're learning."

Young children learn best when they are having fun and bubble play provides opportunities to develop many skills that will help a child at school. Physical, social, attention and communication skills can all be explored through activities with bubbles.

Children will be happy to repeat the activities below regularly, practising skills and strengthening the muscles involved as they have fun. Many of the ideas below can be used indoors or outside but be aware of slippery floors!

- Use shop bought or homemade bubble mixture. Adding a little glycerine to washing up liquid or bubble bath can make bubbles last longer.
- Shaping the mouth and blowing strengthens mouth and lip muscles. These muscles are vital in developing clear speech and sound production.
- It can be difficult initially to control the length, strength and direction of blowing to produce bubbles using a wand. Try holding handfuls of foam for children to blow. Children often blow in an upward direction so holding foam high can achieve success before gradually moving it lower to challenge and develop their oro-motor skills.
- Physical and attention skills can be developed in a number of ways. Ask children to point to bubbles as they float through the air. Learning to isolate one finger to point will help to develop the fine motor skills necessary for handwriting.
- Clapping to pop bubbles helps children to develop their coordination and spatial awareness.

Teaching tip

Children will need to wait their turn and be aware of the feelings of others during this style of play. Talk about desired behaviour before you begin an activity. Do not ask children to blow bubbles for too long, they may get dizzy!

Involving parents

Many of the activities described can be recreated at bath time. Let parents know about the learning benefits and encourage them to play with bubbles too!

Water tray learning

"They love playing in the water. I try to change the toys in there but I'm not always sure what to put in."

We all recognise that young children learn through play and that they don't compartmentalise their learning into separate subject areas. Water play can provide opportunities for cross-curricular learning.

The following ideas show the way in which careful rotation of play resources in a water tray can support learning across the curriculum.

- Personal, Social and Emotional Development: Long tubes that need to be held by more than one child, together with funnels and jugs, encourage children to work collaboratively. Children can be taught to help each other to put on aprons. Self-care can be practised and discussed by carefully bathing dolls, brushing their teeth and drying them on a towel.
- Communication and Language: Play alongside children to encourage them to verbalise their observations and ideas. Model new, often descriptive, vocabulary and encourage children to direct your play and experimentation. Encourage listening by exploring sounds using water poured from watering cans onto tins, dripping water into the tray or pouring water from different heights.
- Physical Development: Developing control over pouring from a jug or bottle can be facilitated by selecting vessels that fit the hands of small children. The use of small fishing nets encourages children to explore distance and develop their spatial awareness.
- Literacy: Plastic or laminated letters, names or words can float in water to be caught in

a small net. Bath crayons often work well on the sides of water trays. Work with the children to write water words that can be displayed near the tray.

- Maths: Boats with numbers written on them can be used to encourage children to make sets by placing the correct number of plastic figures or animals on them. Numbers written under plastic ducks can be used for matching. Volume and capacity can be explored with jugs and bottles.
- Expressive Arts and Design: Recreate familiar situations and encourage children to bath dollies, wash clothes or wash plastic dishes and cutlery. Use water outside to create a car wash or to water plastic or real flowers.
- Understanding of the World: Provide jugs of water with different colour food colourings. Children can observe and describe changes in colour as they mix together. Put a box of different materials next to the tray to explore the texture when dry and then wet or the resulting floating or sinking. Put large blocks of ice in the tray to explore temperature and its effects. Small world toys, such as animals and people, can encourage simple story telling.

Involving parents

Share ideas for water play with parents for use at bath time. Ask them to provide feedback about favourite kinds of water play and incorporate these into your setting.

Taking it further

Consider adding Gelli-Baff, food colouring, bubbles or perfumes to extend water play.

Learning with sand

"He always plays in the sand. I try to get him to do something else so that he can learn different things."

Many children love to play in the sand tray and will choose to spend extended periods of time there each day. By varying the resources available, children will be able to extend their learning to explore all areas of the curriculum.

Teaching tip

While some Early Years settings have large sit-in sand pits, others only have small sand trays. It may be necessary to limit the number of children using the sand at any one time or more sand could be made available. Large tyres can be lined to hold sand, large plastic boxes and even washing-up bowls can be used for some sand play. Sometimes a shallow tray, with only a small amount of sand can promote a different style of play.

The following ideas demonstrate some of the possible ways of exploring different areas of the curriculum through the creative use of sand. Many of the ideas could be adapted to fit in with particular topics.

- Personal, Social and Emotional Development: Spades, large sieves, spoons and bags promote cooperation and encourage children to work together. Providing a variety of items, but only one of each, will encourage children to negotiate turns and challenge children to manage their feelings.
- Communication and Language: Introduce new vocabulary through joining in with sand play. Model language that relates to exploration and investigation such as 'I wonder what will happen if...'. Listen to interactions between children to inform your next steps planning for individual children.
- Physical Development: By providing a variety of different sized spoons and pots children will begin to moderate the physical effort required to lift and control items loaded with wet or dry sand. Large tweezers can be used to pick small items out of the sand, helping to develop a pincer or pencil grip. Mark making in the sand using a paintbrush or stick will improve control over singlehanded tools. Moulding wet sand will increase hand strength.

- Literacy: Laminated letters, words or names can be hidden in the sand. Small plastic figures or animals can link to favourite books to invite story telling. Shallow, dry sand in a tray can be used to practise letter formation.
- Maths: Hide numbers or shapes in the sand and place others on the side of the tray to invite matching. Place coloured saucers next to the tray and small coloured bricks, animals or beads to invite sorting. Pots of different sizes help to teach about volume and capacity.
- Expressive Arts and Design: Wide-toothed combs, rakes, sticks, rollers and biscuit cutters can be used to explore mark making in wet and dry sand. Dry sand, sieves and biscuit tins or drums can be used to make sounds. Sand mixed with water to a dripping consistency can create lovely patterns. Mix with glue and drip onto paper for a more permanent image.
- Understanding of the World: Dry sand can be used with water wheels and funnels. Allow children to mix water into the dry sand to explore the effects. Encourage children to talk about their own experiences by recreating a beach area. Discuss habitats of animals and other countries when playing with desert animals.

Taking it further

There are a variety of coloured and sculpting sands available that could be used in tabletop or adult-led activities. These could be used to motivate some children to try something new and may help build concentration and attention skills.

Bonus idea

Try using sand in story telling. The sand can be used to become a desert island with buried treasure or a landscape that changes as the story progresses. A hill can soon be changed into the banks of a river or beach.

Making more of minibeasts

"He spent ages watching a line of ants. He was the most engaged I have ever seen him."

Arranging trips to farms and zoos isn't always easy but minibeasts can be just as fascinating and can be found in all Early Years environments.

- Consider how ants and bees work together. Discuss caring for minibeasts in their natural environment and talk about the safety issues of touching wasps and bees. Discuss feelings or fears about minibeasts.
- Listen to the sounds that some minibeasts make. Learn nursery rhymes and songs relating to minibeasts. Think of words to describe the appearance, the movements and the feel of worms, slugs and snails. Explore alliteration: slimy snail, active ants, wiggly worms, busy bees.
- Before collecting minibeasts practise picking up rice grains and dried couscous in different ways such as with tweezers, a paintbrush or with fingers. Discuss which method would be most gentle. Get the whole group moving like minibeasts, slow like snails, fast like flies or all in a long line like centipedes.
- Write invitations to 'The Ugly Bug Ball' or create instructions on how to care for snails, caterpillars and spiders.
- Group pictures of minibeasts according to the number of legs, their colour, or the movements they make. Make two-dimensional shape pictures. Make simple pictograms of the beasts you find. Use language relating to size to describe them.
- Describe and compare habitats. Consider the importance of minibeasts. Find out about simple life cycles. Make a menu for a minibeast café.

Windy weather

"You can always tell when it's windy. The children get so excited.
It's difficult to get them to focus on anything."

**The weather does seem to affect the behaviour of young children
and so always be ready to adapt your planning to suit the
conditions. Windy weather can be used to engage children in
making observations and exploratory play.**

The following ideas are generally quick to
prepare and some of the resources could be
stored in a Windy Weather Box ready for the
perfect conditions. If your outside area is small
then some activities could be taken to a local
park or beach.

- Hang ribbons or strips of fabric onto a string
  and watch them when there is no wind, a
  little wind or strong wind. Draw pictures or
  take photos of what you see and discuss the
  differences.
- Listen to the wind. You may hear it flapping
  fabric, blowing a wind chime, or even
  blowing down a chimney. Try to recreate
  the sounds using dried beans on a tray or
  blowing into a microphone.
- Watch leaves blowing in the autumn.
  Children will enjoy throwing them in the air
  and watching them. Ask children to predict
  where they will land.
- Hang a spiral cut from a thin sheet of card
  outside in light wind. Watch it turn. Hang
  another over a radiator and another in
  a space where the air is still. Discuss the
  movement seen and the possible reasons for
  this.
- Make simple boats using plastic tubs, two
  straws or pencils for the mast and a piece
  of carrier bag for a sail. The mast can be
  secured with a lump of play dough. Watch
  boats move on a water tray outside.

Bonus idea ★

For an instant kite, tie
string to the handles
of a thin carrier bag. If
you find it difficult to
keep the bag open to
catch the wind, place
an inflated balloon
inside or a piece
of card across the
opening.

Rainy days

"I think it's too wet to go outside today."

If children and adults are dressed appropriately, playing in the rain can not only be fun, but can also support most areas of the Early Years curriculum. Children can run, jump and stamp in puddles as well as look, feel and mix.

Teaching tip

As the weather can never be relied upon for planning, it can be easier to have a Wet Weather Box ready to use as the opportunity arises. In addition to glitter, flour and umbrellas, you could include a simple, homemade 'rain gauge', made using a funnel and a clear plastic bottle with coloured elastic bands that can be moved to mark the level of the water.

The ideas that follow provide wet weather experiences that promote spontaneous and descriptive language and allow children to make first hand observations.

- Have wellies and waterproof trousers and coats readily available.
- Encourage children to recognise the weather conditions and identify the appropriate clothing.
- Provide items that can be sprinkled onto and mixed into puddles. Small amounts of glitter will float and swirl, powder paint will sit on the surface of a puddle for a while and can be mixed in, flour can create sticky goo that can be dragged with a stick to leave marks. All of these encourage children to look at the result of their actions and promote independent exploration.
- Stand under umbrellas or plastic shelters to listen to the sound of the raindrops. Later, encourage children to recreate these sounds in the water tray or using rice on containers, by tapping their fingers and making shakers.
- Paint outside in the rain. The paper may rip after a while, but the colours will bleed together and run.
- When the rain has stopped and the ground around puddles is dry, explore possible mark making opportunities such as riding bikes, sweeping or dragging sticks.

Outside in spring

"Spring is such a lovely season but how can I make the most of it with the children?"

There are many outdoor learning opportunities in spring. Children who develop an interest in the world around them, looking at things in detail and asking questions, will be able to transfer these learning skills to other situations as they progress through school.

Many of these ideas can be adapted to suit the outside space available. Following the introduction of an idea, observe the responses of the children in order to develop it further and build on their interests.

- Spring is a great time for a minibeast hunt.
- Try planting sweet peas or lavender to attract butterflies and bees.
- Go on a rainbow hunt. Colour each of the sections of some egg boxes a different colour and encourage children to collect small natural items to match the colours. Which were easy or difficult to find?
- Look for textures. More able children could develop their language and observation skills by searching for flexible grasses, rigid bark, gritty soil, furry moss or soggy leaves.
- Look for signs of animals. Children may find a nibbled leaf, a feather, an eggshell or a footprint in mud. Talk to children about these and think about what the animal was doing to leave the evidence. Become nature detectives!
- Copy animals in spring. Build a nest, wiggle through tunnels, collect soft materials or dig holes.
- Plant seeds to watch them grow and change.
- A fresh twig with buds will sprout leaves if placed in water.

Involving parents

Ask parents to help their child to identify the signs of spring near their own homes. You could put a list of things to look for near your entrance for children to tick when they have seen the item.

Outside in summer

"I love the flowers and plants in the summer. The children will have a quick look but then they seem to lose interest."

Children often love to work and play outside and, with a little support, will adapt their play to explore the seasonal changes. The interest and ability to make sense of the changing world around them will support their scientific enquiry at school.

The following ideas could be concentrated into a single day trip or spread throughout the summer in your outside area. Children will use their observation skills to develop an interest in the natural world.

- Make a viewfinder (a piece of card with a 10-20cm square hole or tie sticks into a square for a more natural approach). Encourage children to place their viewfinder in different locations to isolate a small area and see what is there. Alternatively, hold viewfinders at arm's length to appreciate different views. Try looking up into a tree or through a gap in a hedge.
- Draw attention to shadows. Look at the shapes and lengths. You could play a game in which you try to stop others from treading on your own shadow.
- Try to find a minibeast and follow its path. A line of ants will be fun to track or point to a butterfly or bee as it moves around. Where have they been and where are they going?
- Stop and listen to the sounds around you.
- You could work in groups to set up and follow trails of flowers or sticks laid as arrows.
- Make a pictorial list of things to find. Children could work in pairs or in a group and tick off items as they are found.

Bonus idea ★

Try using a dandelion flower sap as magic ink. Simply break off a flower and use the sap from the stem to make marks on paper. While the marks will be difficult to see initially, they will become clear as the sap dries.

Outside in autumn

"We always collect leaves and look at the colours, but what else can we do outside in autumn?"

After the ease of playing outside in the summer without coats and wellies, it can be tempting to move indoors as the autumn winds blow. But autumn offers many learning opportunities to use our senses to find out about the natural world.

Children can experience things outside that they won't find inside and some children will find outside discovery more motivating than inside activities. If you have limited access to a natural environment, it would be possible to collect some of the resources to work with them in whatever outside area you may have.

- Try to look for squirrels and watch them. If the squirrels aren't keen to stay near a noisy group, you could watch short video clips on a computer first! Encourage children to think about why the squirrels hide their acorns and then ask children to copy them. Ask children to think of ways to remember where they have hidden their acorn. Can they find it again at the end of your walk?
- Encourage children to smell blackberries, apples and even bark and leaves. Mash items with a little water to increase the scent.
- Make leaf belts, bracelets or hats. Take strips of card with double-sided tape to create a basic frame and encourage children to collect leaves to attach. You could give a child a particular colour to collect or allow a free choice.
- Listen to the variety of sounds and record them to identify later. Crunching through leaves, squelching in mud and splashing in puddles all make distinct sounds. Try to go outside to listen to the rain falling on leaves, umbrellas, or puddles and the wind blowing.

Taking it further

Talk about a book character or imaginary animal that wants to stay dry in the woods. You could collect sticks, bracken and leaves to build a shelter. Check the next day to see if it's still standing.

Outside in winter

"The children get so cold outside we don't often stay out for long."

When dressed correctly, children can enjoy playing and learning outside and will begin to recognise the patterns in seasonal changes. The contrasts between outside and inside temperatures can be used to promote investigations and observation skills.

Teaching tip

Young children can get cold quickly. Ensure that children are dressed appropriately and try to keep them engaged in physically active play. Build up a collection of spare hats and gloves for children who arrive without warm clothes.

The following ideas aim to draw attention to, and interest children in, the changes to trees, animals and temperatures during the winter months.

- When looking at trees in winter, show children photos of trees with leaves to draw attention to the differences.
- Collect small branches with twigs and weave wool and string between some of the twigs and around the branches. These can be displayed by hanging them outside.
- When temperatures drop below freezing try putting some ice outside and some inside. Look at the changes at regular intervals and encourage children to describe and explain these.
- Make ice art by pouring water into a shallow tray. Add a string loop that will be used to hang your work. Select and place leaves, twigs, stones or food colouring into the water and leave to freeze. Hang your ice art outside, near a window where children can observe the changes.
- Collect pinecones. Children will enjoy decorating these with glitter, paint or scrunched paper forced into the open spaces.

Working together

Part 11

Cooperation games

"Some of the children just don't seem to be part of the group."

Seeing themselves as part of the group, recognising that they have a role to play and learning to be aware of their peers can help children learn to cooperate with others.

Teaching tip

Using phrases such as 'we are going to work together to...' helps children to recognise the benefit of cooperating with others.

These activities require little or no preparation and children will enjoy repeating the games, increasing in confidence as they become familiar with the rules and expectations.

- Try playing paired mirror games, in which one child takes the lead to make large, slow movements while their partner copies. These games encourage children to pay attention to their partner and develop awareness of their own body.
- In a defined space, ask children to walk around without touching anyone else. Next, ask children to hold the hand of a partner and repeat. The group lengths can increase, making the challenge more difficult. Children will develop their spatial awareness and begin to consider other children when making choices about movement.
- 'Get Knotted' is a simple game in which children hold hands in a circle. One child passes under the arms of others, followed by another creating a knot. You could have one child who directs the others on where to move in order to undo the knot. They need to be aware that fast or strong movements are likely to result in the chain being broken.
- Build a group machine. Begin by asking one child to select a movement and sound that can be repeated. Gradually add more children to the machine, each choosing a different sound and action, increasing the size and volume until all children are involved.

Taking it further

Combine these activities with music for added interest, and if possible video activities so that children can see themselves as part of the whole.

Tidy up time

"They just put the toys anywhere! It's easier to tidy up myself."

Jigsaws with missing pieces and construction toys with pieces that don't fit are an irritation to all Early Years workers. Teach children to take care of toys and resources, to work together to put them away and to behave while doing so.

These ideas help to calm children down at tidy up time and speed up this essential part of the day while also providing opportunities to practise basic skills.

- Ensure that time to 'stop play' and to 'tidy up' is clearly signalled. Playing music helps to indicate this change and can also be calming.
- Maths and science skills of matching and sorting can be practised when tidying mixed toys. As with all simple sorting, make criteria clear by sticking photos of the toys on the sides of the boxes, both inside and out. Be aware that some children will not yet have developed sorting skills. Simplify the activity by identifying one or two particular items that should be collected.
- Stick silhouettes of the resources on shelves to indicate where they live and to highlight what is missing.
- In a large setting, groups of children with their key worker can take responsibility for a small area each day. Reducing the area will help less able children to learn where to put things and working with a key worker allows opportunities to make observations.
- When enthusiasm begins to wane, start a countdown to indicate that time is nearly up.
- Ensure that children know where to go once the room and outside area are tidy.

Teaching tip

Award stickers for good tidying. If some children are reluctant to help, look out for small attempts and praise these efforts.

Bonus idea ★

Naming a special helper for the day or for the week can help children to accept and enjoy responsibility.

In it together

"Look what **we** did!"

Learning to play with a common purpose sets the foundations for successful co-learning situations that will be encountered in school. Give consideration to the available resources and activities, together with the layout of the rooms in your setting to encourage collaborative work and play.

Teaching tip

Simple challenges can be a good way to encourage collaborative work. Children could try to pass a satsuma from one spoon to another, place a pasta tube on a straw held by another child or take turns to thread beads onto a thread as quickly as possible.

Bonus idea ★

Pairing children together as helpers encourages them to share responsibilities and to work together. It can be a good way to introduce the role to a new or less confident child.

- Work with small groups of children on a common, open-ended creative task. Make sure that you are at the same height as the children and model listening and questioning. It is good to mix the abilities within these groups as the able children will practise and develop their skills attempting to engage with the less able who will learn from their peer modelling.
- Encourage children to work on shared creative projects. It can be difficult to share a painting, but printmaking and model making can be much more successful.
- Introduce ongoing large-scale collages, in which everyone can be involved. When complete, use the image to encourage speaking and listening skills. Ask children about their involvement and emphasise the advantages of having worked together.
- Set short, fun challenges, for example building towers of bricks. Encourage children to take turns to add bricks to the pile. Extend this activity for more able children by giving them different coloured bricks and then discussing the patterns created.
- Re-enact simple familiar stories with each child taking on a different role. Simple story telling through drama relies on individuals performing their role and an awareness of others within the group. Ensure that less confident children have a less demanding role and offer any necessary support.

Outside together

"Look what **we** can do!"

Learning to work collaboratively on large-scale projects or physical activities combines work in all three of the EYFS prime areas and develops skills that can be transferred to many learning situations.

Safety needs to be considered but it is commonly believed that some controlled risk-taking teaches children to make their own informed judgements. Children may need to be encouraged to participate, to listen to others or to persevere, but all children, whatever their ability, can benefit from working together.

Teaching tip

If outside space is a problem, you could plan a trip to the park, the woods or the beach to focus on collaborative play.

- When selecting new toys, consider whether they encourage collaboration. Some bikes are made for two or can have a trolley attached behind, small seesaws demand collaboration, telephone talking tubes and large, handled ball-rolling trays require two children to work together.
- Adult-led activities can be challenging and fun. A ribbon with rings threaded on it can be wound around trees and through hoops, then ask two children to hold onto a ring and move it from one end of the ribbon to the other without letting go. Pull and push a large ball in a pillowcase around a simple obstacle course in a pair. Large cardboard boxes provide endless opportunities and can be used for just one day if storage is a problem.
- Guttering can be used to roll balls or cars down. Children can take turns to roll or catch.
- Encourage children to help each other to balance along low equipment.
- If two children are digging in the sand, encourage them to join their holes together.
- Observe the physical, verbal and non-verbal interaction between children.

Bonus idea

Thread a small hoop or tube onto a rope or pole. Encourage children to raise and lower the ends to make the hoop or tube move from one child to the other.

Sitting in circles

"We often sit in a circle to sing but I'm not sure what else we could do."

Sitting in a circle is a lovely way for children to learn many social skills. Each child is able to see the others and observe their facial expressions and body language as well as hear their responses.

Teaching tip

Try to sit less confident children next to a familiar adult in the circle. If a child is not able to take their turn unaided, the adult will be able to support them subtly, without drawing attention to them.

The following ideas require little or no preparation. Group sizes and the duration of the session can be varied to suit the age and concentration of the children. Adults sitting in the circle should also take their turn to model actions and responses.

- Begin a session with a reasonably fast action that can be passed around the circle from one person to the next. This could be passing a smile or clapping the syllables in each name. The children will not have to wait too long initially and will learn that everyone will have a turn.
- Introduce a microphone or another small object that can be passed around the circle to indicate whose turn it is to speak. If a child doesn't want to take a turn, allow them to pass the microphone on to the next child.
- Children need to learn to listen to the person who is speaking. This can be encouraged by asking children to take turns to give a simple instruction that others should follow.
- Explore emotions by passing an expression such as happy, sad, cross or excited around the circle and then take turns to say something that makes them feel that way.
- Objects can be passed around the circle, slowly initially and then faster. You could introduce more than one object to encourage children to move the focus of their attention from one place to another.

Activities and abilities

"Sometimes it is difficult to make the activity simple enough for the less able children while still keeping it interesting for the others."

The following ideas could be applied to a variety of free choice or adult-led activities and focus largely on extending or supporting attention, speaking and listening skills.

To reduce the complexity of the activity:

- Repeat instructions, allowing time for processing.
- Draw attention to visual information, for example, if you are referring to objects, gesture towards them as you use their name, if you are referring to actions, model them as you speak.
- Reduce the number of key words used in a short sentence.
- Begin with the simplest questions.

To extend activities for the more able children:

- Reduce the amount of gesture used alongside familiar language.
- Possibly remove some of the visual information, encouraging a greater dependence on listening.
- Select less familiar objects.
- Increase the number and variety of objects.
- Add a time delay between the words and action to extend the ability to recall information. For example, 'after we have... we will...'.
- Include a concept, possibly position or size.
- Increase the difficulty of question words used. Who? Which? What will...? When? Why? How?

> **Teaching tip**
>
> New staff and volunteers may find it helpful to have a list of ways to differentiate activities displayed in the working area. This may have the added effect of improving the relevance of some ongoing observations.

Look and learn

"Displays take so long to put up. It hardly seems worth it."

In school, children will have a variety of information displayed around the classroom to support their learning. Children who show an interest in displays will be able to identify and use this information with greater independence.

It can be difficult to make displays that maintain the interest of young children. Most children are used to screens with moving images and sound. Below are some ideas that may help engage and maintain their interest.

- Where possible, place displays at child height rather than above their sight line.
- Try to make displays interactive with flaps to lift or lines to follow.
- Where possible, include sensory experiences. Perfume can be added to spring displays and textured papers or fabrics included in animal displays.
- Make your display focus clear but use children's interests to draw them to look. If you are working on numbers, you could hide trains, television characters or animals behind flaps with numbers. Children will be motivated to look for favourite images.
- Once a new display is up, make time to look at it with the children, demonstrating the possibilities.
- Promote writing by including clear, handwritten labels. It is tempting to use printed text because it looks neater, but some handwritten words help children to appreciate the importance of writing.
- When planning a display, consider the different abilities of the children within the group.

Bonus idea ★

If all display boards in your room are high, place display tables beneath for hands-on work and include strings or ribbons that lead to the display above, drawing the child's attention to the board.

Wow! Well done!

"We put the children's work up but they hardly ever look at it and don't seem too bothered."

Promoting pride in work is vital to inspire children to try their best, and a well thought out display can help children to value their own work and show an interest in the work produced by their peers.

By putting work on a special display, children will learn to recognise that other people value their attempts and effort.

- Allow children to have an input into the selection of work to go on display.
- Ensure that all children's work is shown at some time. It is easy to overlook the immature scribble, but if that has taken effort it should be appreciated.
- Try to include examples of children's early independent writing. Although it may not be accurate, or even recognisable, it is important that young children continue to attempt to work independently rather than relying on adult support.
- Once a display is created, ask children for their ideas for captions and write these by hand in front of the children. You could include 'Sophie says...' writing comments in speech bubbles.
- Display three-dimensional work at child height. Captions can be written on folded card. If using a table, children will enjoy decorating it with stars or tinsel to show that it is special.
- Include photos of any temporary work such as castles made of bricks, nests made of twigs or snow sculptures.
- Collaboration can be recognised by adding a 'we worked together' star next to these items.

Teaching tip

Try to change the work on display regularly. This will allow more work to be seen, give children an ongoing sense of pride and achievement, and will generate a greater interest in the display. Encourage children to show their parents or carers when their work is displayed.

Bonus idea ★

Outdoor displays may not last long but an area could be set aside and decorated for children to place natural artwork.

Trips out

"The trips are good but they take a lot of time to organise and some parents never pay."

Trips out with groups of children can be expensive and involve pages of risk assessments. They are, however, extremely valuable. Children are able to learn from real experiences and will learn to transfer their knowledge to other situations.

Teaching tip

Always check that you have permission from parents and guardians to take children off site and ensure that all risks have been considered. Short trips on a regular basis will have a greater impact on a child's understanding of the world around them than one long expensive trip.

Taking it further

If possible, when you are in local shops, allow children to buy small items, for example, something that may be used for a cookery session. Draw children's attention to the exchange of money for an item, the use of the till and the use of words like please and thank you. Remind children of their experiences when introducing role-play shops.

It's not always necessary to plan expensive trips. Consider arranging local trips that look at manmade features in your local area.

- Many children travel by car and rarely walk around their local area. Short walks with small groups of children allow time to look at, and talk about, features of the local manmade environment.
- Have a focus to your walk and ensure that the adults and children are aware of this before setting off.
- You could look for uses of technology in the local area. Help children to take photos of traffic lights, crossings, street lights, and parking meters. Talk about their use and when they are on and off.
- Look for street furniture. Name, describe and discuss who might use the benches, post boxes and signs.
- Look at local shops. What do they sell? Are they busy?
- Look at types of buildings. Discuss the different uses of houses, shops, churches, offices and public buildings.
- Look at doors, in particular look at the numbers on them, their size and colour, letter boxes and count the steps that lead up to them.

Hearing from home

"Some of the parents want to talk about their child for hours, others just drop them off and go. It's tricky to get the balance."

Involvement in a child's education by parents and carers can make a huge impact on their achievements and the earlier that this begins the better.

Parents and carers can provide invaluable information about their child's interests and abilities that can help engage and support their development throughout their early years. In a busy Early Years environment, it can be difficult to find the time to meet with parents regularly and to nurture relationships with parents who are reluctant to engage with the setting. These ideas help to encourage parents to play an active role in their child's early years education.

- Photos of staff, together with their name and role, can help parents to feel more comfortable about approaching a member of the team. Place these near the entrance or waiting area.
- If possible, arrange times when parents are invited to play and learn alongside their children. Parents will develop an understanding of the way in which you work and will be more aware of opportunities for similar learning at home.
- Parents who have negative memories of their school days are less likely to want to become involved. It will take time to build trust.
- Parents need to be made aware that their comments and observations are vital in building an accurate picture of their child's development. Invite parents to note any progress seen and place it in a Wow box. Try to avoid competition between parents by not making these comments too public.

Teaching tip

Parents and carers may see their child in a very different way to the way in which they are perceived at the setting and it is easy to be sceptical. Parents who report that a child has a particular ability or skill that has not been seen at the setting are unlikely to be trying to deceive you. Work with parents to gain an accurate picture of the child.